if nobody loves you

# CREATE

## THE DEMAND

# THE FREEMAN INSTITUTE®

FreemanInstitute.com

## FIVE ARENAS OF EXPERTISE

I.   Workshop / Seminar / Retreat Facilitation / Keynote Addresses

II.  Reality-Based Organizational Culture Change

III. Executive Success Coaching / Critical Incident Debriefings

IV.  Diversity & Cultural Competency / Black History

V.   Entrepreneurship / Creative Business Implementation

---

To Book Dr. Freeman
(see pages 199-202)

# GET YOUR ENTREPRENEURIAL JUICES FLOWING!

"I was a one-time runaway and juvenile delinquent. Fast-forward fourteen years. As a bestselling novelist and the owner of my own book publishing company, we have sold over one million books independently and have been a part of generating over twelve million dollars in the marketplace. None of it has been easy. I worked hard until success found me. That's why I like this book. **It's not for the faint of heart.** It tells it like it is—at street level. **No smoke. No mirrors.** Dr. Joel Freeman has done **a masterful job** of taking complex issues and breaking them down into easy-to-implement, bite-sized chunks of **entrepreneurial wisdom. This insightful book is a gem,** well worth your time."

— TERI WOODS

Publisher and Author, *True to the Game*—TeriWoodsPublishing.com

"Each year millions of people think about starting their own entrepreneurial pursuits. Joel Freeman's **refreshingly to-the-point book is an essential guide** for those who possess the courage <u>and</u> the drive to follow their dreams."

— STEVE FORBES

President and CEO of Forbes, Inc., Editor-in-Chief, *Forbes* Magazine, US Presidential Candidate, 1996 and 2000—Forbes.com

"In this **easy-to-read book**, Joel Freeman has made a point that I have always stressed; namely, that the person who has the most to do with what happens to you is *YOU*. When people understand their own potential, the sky is the limit. *If Nobody Loves You, Create the Demand* will help you explore your potential, enhancing the quality of your entrepreneurial journey. There's **not a wasted word in this informative, power-packed book!**"

— BENJAMIN S. CARSON, SR., M.D.

Director of Pediatric Neurosurgery, Johns Hopkins Hospital—DrBenCarson.com

"Over the years I have read a lot of books on similar topics. But **this book stands out.** Freeman has done an exceptional job of combining **practical advice, personal vulnerability, and evocative content**—without wasting a single word. A compelling read! **If you have an entrepreneurial itch to scratch, this is the book for you.**"

— JOSEPH GUERRIERO

Publisher of *Success* Magazine—SuccessMagazine.com

"Cha-Ching! Find an hour or two and read this entire book now! Joel Freeman's **entrepreneurial wisdom, advice, and secrets** really can put thousands of new dollars in your pocket within ninety days. . . . I guarantee. It's **the shortest and best book I've read** on the subject in years. Thank you, Joel, for creating a gem and sharing your success with us. It's a **micro masterpiece.**"

— GEORGE FRASER

Author, *Success Runs In Our Race*—FraserNet.com

"Dr. Joel Freeman's *If Nobody Loves You, Create the Demand* is a **blueprint for success** for any entrepreneur, business owner, and professional. This masterpiece outlines Joel's personal experience in business and gives practical advice to help any business or individual excel. In one insightful book, Joel captures over thirty years of lessons, strategies, and techniques he learned from his personal career and other senior professionals. In fact, **if I had this book when I started my career, Joel's concepts would have saved me time, stress, and money.** . . . Mind-blowing methods and out-of-the-box suggestions are throughout the book to help you get your business off the ground. . . . Usually authors as intelligent as Dr. Freeman write a philosophical book that is hard to make sense out of, however, *If Nobody Loves You, Create the Demand* is **a well-written, praiseworthy manuscript that will change the way I will do business.** I will caution you: once you read this book, there are **no more excuses.** This **brilliant piece of work** makes operating a business or pursuing your entrepreneur itch much easier. . . . Go and make this your year even *If Nobody Loves You . . . Create the Demand.*"

— LES BROWN

National/International Motivational Speaker and Coach—LesBrown.com

"A **very good book** that should be read by the **serious marketer**."

— PETER SHEA

Chairman/CEO, *Entrepreneur* Magazine—Entrepreneur.com

"Your life and your success are in your own hands; this book, *If Nobody Loves You, Create the Demand*, **shows you how to get behind the wheel to your future**."

— BRIAN TRACY

Author, *The Way To Wealth*—BrianTracy.com

"*If Nobody Loves You, Create the Demand* by Joel Freeman is an energy filled book which **shares secrets on how to be a successful entrepreneur**. A fun read you shouldn't miss."

— KEN BLANCHARD

Co author, *The One Minute Manager* and *The Secret*—KenBlanchard.com

"I love the way Joel Freeman leaves out the parts readers skip. In the midst of dynamic stories, this book overflows with **solid, time-proven truths that will revolutionize your life**, your home, and your work. Don't just buy this book. Buy four and give them away!"

— PHIL CALLAWAY

Popular speaker and best-selling author of *Laughing Matters*—PhilCallaway.com

"*If Nobody Loves You, Create the Demand* should be **required reading for every would-be entrepreneur** who asks the question: "How do I succeed in business?" Such a text is **invaluable to the novice** and a **great refresher for the seasoned professional**. Dr. Joel Freeman has created an **authentic, frank, to-the-point guide that will put dollars in your pocket and creative ideas in your head**. All you have to do is follow his wise suggestions!"

— CAROLYN CORBIN

President, Center for the 21st Century. Author, *Great Leaders See the Future First*—c21c.com

"I am certainly no stranger to the successes and failures (and successful failures) of being a small business owner. I have been a successful composer/songwriter (over 2000 written, over 600 recorded, and over 150 chart hits), arranger/artist (Grammy's and Dove, BMI, ASCAP awards), studio owner (13), label(s) owner, publishing company owner (8), producer of over 2000 artists—with such rock hits as 'Cherry Pie,' 'Alley-Oop,' 'Monster Mash' (3 time hit), 'Woman, Sensuous Woman' (3 time country and pop hit), and Gospel standard, 'He Was There All The Time' (recorded over 100 times worldwide in many languages)—in total have been involved in selling over 100,000,000 records. I am truly astounded that an author of Dr. Freeman's class, expertise, and international influence would choose one of my hit song titles, 'If Nobody Loves You, Create The Demand' for the title of his latest book. If this **brilliant book** had been available to me from 1955 through 1993, I would have received and been able to keep some of the countless millions that should have come my way. This **book of common sense wisdom** would have helped me immensely. It is a **burst of constant, how-to-do-it-right information** with credibility and integrity from cover to cover."

— GARY S. PAXTON

Composer, songwriter, record label owner—GarySPaxton.org

"Joel Freeman has a **novel perspective on success and the meaning of life**. I learned a great deal from this book, and you will too. Don't miss it!"

— ROGER DAWSON

Author, *Secrets of Power Negotiating*—Rdawson.com

"I live vicariously through smart books like Dr. Joel Freeman's, *If Nobody Loves You, Create The Demand*. I could never write like him but I can apply his wisdom and insight. This **new book takes a fresh approach to an age old challenge**—how can an average person stand out and compete in a world of, seemingly, superstars? Today just knowing you need to be in demand accelerates your journey to a successful life."

— MIKE SMITH

President, Michael Smith and Associates—MichaelSmithandAssociates.com

"This book is **uniquely dynamic. Like lightning in a bottle.** Read it—along with responding to the *creative thinking* questions at the end of each chapter. It will **ignite or re-ignite your entrepreneurial passion like few other books I have read.** I spent most of the reading of this book kicking myself for all the times that I found myself saying, 'That's right.' I look forward to sharing this publication with friends who, like myself, have stopped being assertive about the talent and dreams that are a part of us all. My ancestors shared a dream of freedom with each generation that they touched, which is why there is a little Kunta Kinte, Chicken George and Queen in all of us. They had the courage and conviction to act and create a dream."

— WILLIAM ALEXANDER HALEY
CEO, Alex Haley Family, Inc.—KinteHaley.org

"Amazing! What a gift! As a former executive with Century 21 Real Estate through the unprecedented growth years, I worked with hundreds of entrepreneurs and was acquainted with many books on how to write business plans and draft financials. In the midst of those types of books, *If Nobody Loves You, Create the Demand* **is unique**. It is a valuable resource, filled with **many 'ah-has' and gold nuggets** about how to position your business practice successfully. Joel, thank you for sharing your creativity and insights!"

— DICK EAGAN
President, Dynamic Management

"When I first started in real estate, it was only to subsidize my income from a job I had in corporate America. I could never seem to get to the point where I made enough money. I realized that there was a glass ceiling on how high I could advance. In 2000 I took the big step. I bought my own real estate franchise and have never looked back. **This book is rare.** No fluff. It gets right to the point and never wavers. **I highly recommend it. It's a quick read, but it will take a lifetime to digest.**"

— JANICE CORLEY
President and CEO, Sudler Sotheby's International Realty—SudlerSothebysRealty.com

"Joel Freeman has written a hard hitting book that **will get your entrepreneurial juices flowing**. Read this and get ready to rock the world."

— PAT WILLIAMS

Senior Vice President, NBA Orlando Magic—PatWilliamsMotivate.com

"Here's a book that's a **quick read and a wealth of practical tips** on starting and growing a business. Read it and then go do it!"

— RICH DEVOS

Owner and Chairman, NBA Orlando Magic and Co-Founder of Alticor, Inc., —Alticor.com

"If you have an unwritten symphony in you . . . a great idea for a business, a novel, a seminar . . . this book will press you to either write the symphony or just go back to singing in the shower. If you decide you're ready to write, Joel will lead you from critical step to critical step. **No fat, no fads, no wasted time. A great read!**"

— JOHN CUMMUTA

Author, *Transforming Debt Into Wealth*®—JohnCummuta.com

"**This book will change your life!** Joel's international experience and wealth of knowledge will put you on the **fast track** to personal and professional success. Read it. Believe it. Live it. Enjoy it!"

— BRIAN D. MOLITOR

Author, *The Power of Agreement Unleashed*—PowerOfAgreement.com

"I have read many books by entrepreneurs like Walt Disney, Sam Walton, and Thomas Watson. But *If Nobody Loves You, Create the Demand* is the first entrepreneurial book I have read that **carries wisdom, strategy, and a plan** to accomplish your business goals as it relates to a service. Well done! Thank you, Joel."

— WILLIAM I. KISSINGER, CPA/PFS, CFP

President, Kissinger Financial Services, Inc.—Kissingernet.com

"Upon finishing the reading of *If Nobody Loves You, Create the Demand*, I reflected back on my experiences as an entrepreneur. **I only wish this book was available thirty-five years ago when I began my career as a consultant.** Freeman meticulously outlined, in each chapter, many of the major pitfalls and successes, along with the skills and tools needed to pursue a business in consulting on a limited budget. **I would recommend this book as a guide for anyone going into business for themselves.** Thank you, Joel, for sharing your enthusiasm, insights, and experiences through this book.

— DR. TED PAYNTHER
John Gray Associates


"This practical book is **a 'tell it like it is' collection of insight and wisdom for anyone who is beginning their business—or improving it.** It's a great read from someone who has been there and can speak truth to those who are there."

— THOMAS ADDINGTON, PH.D.
Co-founder and Managing Director of Wellspring Group, Ltd.—WellSpring-Group.com


"Being the founder of America's seventh largest radio broadcasting company didn't come easily. I began my radio career in 1969. At the time, **I wish I had a book like this to read.** I have found it to be **profound, entertaining, and practical.** This book is **a solid guide** for anyone who wants to achieve their business goals. This **book is every entrepreneur's dream.** If you are **looking for a gift** for your son, daughter, grandchild, niece, or nephew, this will help launch them professionally and can provide them a foundation for **a lifetime of personal and career success.**"

— CATHERINE L. HUGHES
Founder, Chairperson of the Board and Secretary, Radio One—Radio-One.com

# RESPONSES FROM READERS OF THE FIRST MANUSCRIPT

"Outstanding! I opened the manuscript to give it quick skim, and **the first page jumped out and seized me**. . . . I couldn't stop until I finished the last word!!! This is classic Joel Freeman . . . **creative, right to the point**, easy to read and digest. Once picked up, it's very hard to put down. I have read it twice, and want to read it again . . ."

". . . This manuscript made me **feel like the author was having a conversation with me** from across the table . . . **gives ordinary people the opportunity to reach their potential** . . . targets adults, but also gives teenagers a forward look to the **building blocks** they will need to be successful in life . . . **not a pie in the sky**. . . . **Years of expertise in a small package** . . ."

". . . As I read the manuscript I **almost felt guilty for being able to get this kind of information without having to pay**. I'm sure this book will be in great demand. I learned so much, and you must know that I plan to use and put into practice some of the nuggets in my own personal life."

"Every school, every mentoring group, every faith-based and every community-based organization **needs to start an Entrepreneur Club**. Entrepreneurial pursuits provide wonderful laboratories for addressing the basic issues of life. This book, with discussion questions at the end of each chapter, **is an excellent resource for any group of people** involved in small business enterprises."

# if nobody loves you
# CREATE
## THE DEMAND

A Powerful Jolt of
Entrepreneurial
Energy and Wisdom

JOEL A. FREEMAN, PH.D.

Authentic

COLORADO SPRINGS • LONDON • HYDERABAD

Authentic Publishing
We welcome your questions and comments.

USA   1820 Jet Stream Drive, Colorado Springs, CO 80921
      www.authenticbooks.com
UK    9 Holdom Avenue, Bletchley, Milton Keynes, Bucks, MK1 1QR
      www.authenticmedia.co.uk
India   Logos Bhavan, Medchal Road, Jeedimetla Village, Secunderabad 500 055, A.P.

If Nobody Loves You, Create the Demand

Please visit our websites for other great titles and ideas:
FreemanInstitute.com
FreemanStuff.com
WorkHardWorkSmart.com

For information regarding author interviews
or speaking at your next event, contact
410-729-4011

It was Gary S. Paxton's hit song title,
"If Nobody Loves You, Create The Demand"
that inspired the title of this book. Thank you, Gary.

A percentage of the royalties from this book will go to
The Freeman Institute® Foundation—FreemanInstituteFoundation.org

Library of Congress Cataloging-in-Publication Data

Freeman, Joel A., 1954-
    If nobody loves you, create the demand : a powerful jolt of entrepreneurial energy and wisdom / Joel A. Freeman.
      p. cm.
    ISBN-13: 978-1-932805-98-7 (pbk.)
    1. Entrepreneurship. 2. New business enterprises. 3. Success in business. I. Title.
    HD62.5.F73 2007
    658.4'21--dc22
                        2007015765

Cover design: Paul Lewis
Interior design: Angela Lewis
Editorial team: KJ Larson, Dana Carrington

Printed in the United States of America

# LESSONS FROM A TRACTOR

### Dedicated to
### Fred and Flora Weeks

---

I worked for two summers on Fred and Flora's dairy farm in Litchfield, Maine in 1968 and 1969 when I was fourteen and fifteen years of age. Everyday I helped carry large pails of milk and record the weight of the milk from each cow during the milkings at four o'clock in the morning and four o'clock in the afternoon. The late mornings and early afternoons were spent haying, gardening, cutting timber, or doing general farm work. The first summer I received ten dollars a week, plus room and board. The next summer I got a raise, twenty-five dollars a week.

Fred was an easy-going man, a remarkable mentor in his own way. I remember one day I got the hare-brained idea that I would spruce up the old grease-it-before-you-use-it Farmall tractor. Big wheels on the rear and small tires, about a foot apart, on the front. It was begging for a coat of paint. So I asked if I could slap some paint on it. Fred explained that the painting process involved sanding the rust off before applying the paint. I nodded in agreement. Sounded simple enough.

Later that day he drove me down to the local hardware store and bought some sandpaper, a brush, and a gallon of fire-engine red high-gloss oil paint. I was thrilled. When we got home I started on the easiest part of the tractor—the large area covering the top and front of the engine. It was easily accessible and relatively rust-free. The sandpaper part of the job was a snap. The paint went on smoothly. It glistened in the afternoon sun. (View pictures of Fred, Flora, and tractor at CreateTheDemand.com.)

I backed off a few yards, surveying the scene. I then did a full 360 degree turn. I looked at the rust all over the spokes on the wheels and on other parts of the tractor with hard-to-reach pits and ridges. It looked nasty and grungy, with dried cow manure caked over some of the rust. There was no way I was going to hug those wheels to get off all that rust.

At that moment I had an epiphany. I decided that I was done with the job. I went to the barn, found the turpentine and cleaned the brush. In my mind, the tractor looked fine. *Heck, it's only going to be used out in the field. We're not talking about a cool looking chick magnet used to cruise the main street on Saturday evenings. No big deal. It's certainly better off than it was . . . it's a tractor, for Pete's sake!*

The next day I went about my business. Fred let a couple of days pass without saying anything about the half-done painting job. I guess he finally figured out that I was done with the tractor, but he wanted to verify it with me. "Joel, when are you planning to finish painting the tractor?" he ventured.

"I'm done," I responded. "I figured that I took the job as far as I could take it." Seemed like a logical response any rational person would understand. *I mean, look at them nasty spokes, would you?*

It was the only time I ever saw Fred get mad. Steam was coming out of his shirt collar. He put the fear of God in me. He never raised his voice, but there was an unmistakable tight-jawed, eye-piercing Clint Eastwood authority. In a controlled, firm manner he said, "Joel, you will finish what you started. Now go get the sandpaper and start working on the wheels."

I experienced more than just hard work that early-to-bed-early-to-rise summer. I learned that it was important to complete a job that I had started, no matter how difficult or boring. I now finish some things that I shouldn't have started in the first place. But that's beside the point.

Flora died a few years ago. Fred died September 26, 2005. He was ninety. I used to call him at least once a month (sometimes more) to see how he was doing. I miss both of them, but especially Fred. Even though I finally cleared his phone number out of my cell phone's memory the other day, his legacy lives on. Here's to the "Freds" and the "Floras" of the world.

# CONTENTS

# CHAPTER ONE

# A MOST FANTASTIC VIEW, FOG PERMITTING

*If your ship doesn't come in, swim out to it!*

Jonathan Winters

*Money and success don't change people;*
*they merely amplify what is already there.*

Will Smith

Have you ever tried to navigate your way through a dense fog or a blinding blizzard? It can be both dangerous and exciting. Growing up in Alberta, Canada, I have encountered a few of those "can't-see-my-outstretched-hand-in-front-of-me" blizzards. I have also driven and walked in dense fog on the coast of Maine. Both types of experiences are challenging on many levels. You're lucky if you can see a few feet ahead of you at any given time.

An entrepreneurial pursuit is somewhat similar—forward motion in a thick fog. The kind of fog that seems to weigh you down,

1

though it weighs nothing. An immensely oppressive and ponderous weight of lightness. You cautiously pace yourself, feeling your way toward an unformed shadow of an idea that initially looked like a promising expenditure of your time, energy, and money.

You know what it's supposed to look like. You once had a fantastic view of it. Whatever *it* is. But when you arrive, what you currently see is really desolate and troublesome—what could be called "destination sickness."

The best laid (business) plans can become fuzzy and out of focus, or can even seem to vanish. It may even seem like you have squandered your limited reserves of time, energy, and finances. You are engaging in the process of going down alleys to see if they go anywhere . . . or if they are blind.

Kind of like a research scientist, propelled by the vision of developing the cure for a ravaging disease or an inventor trying to conceive of something that no other human on the planet has ever imagined. Wernher Von Braun (one of the most important rocket developers and an early champion of space exploration) said, "Research is what I am doing when I don't know what I am doing." Ever felt that way?

## An Entrepreneurial Pursuit and You

Some people just do not have the stomach for this kind of startup work—walking in a fog or going down blind alleys. They want a secure and settled environment complete with benefits, retirement plan, insurance, all systems and protocol in place. There's nothing wrong with that, but you get the picture.

Entrepreneurial pursuits aren't for everybody. If every person stepped out on his or her own, corporations would falter and a nation's economy would suffer. Working in a corporate environment is a noble profession.

In fact, your start-up business may grow to become a secure and settled corporation some day, complete with benefits, retirement plan, insurance, and all the systems and protocol in place. It's just that some people acquire an inconvenient, somewhat maddening entrepreneurial itch that needs scratching. And it's an itch that won't go away with one or two scratches. Are you feeling that itch? If so, this book is for you.

By the way, people do not need to exit their day jobs to become entrepreneurs. Most are "evening executives," "midnight moguls" and/or "weekend merchants"—selling stuff on eBay or some other home-based business that brings in extra cash. Some of those ventures may even become substantial enough a few years from now, inviting that individual to flirt with the idea of quitting his or her day job.

## Purpose of this Book

I am a professional speaker, author, corporate trainer, consultant, and confidential CID coach of senior executives, professional athletes, and entertainers. I realize that much of what I am communicating in this book will reflect my vocation and may have special appeal to performers, seminar facilitators, executive coaches, agents, corporate trainers, network marketers, publicists, writers, film makers, sales people, clergy, inventors, financial planners, professional speakers, business consultants, franchise owners, graphic artists, insurance brokers, entertainers, magicians. . . .

If you don't see your profession listed, do not worry. It's about most professions or products requiring savvy marketing. Understanding the internal world of an entrepreneur is a primary focus of this book, which transcends professions.

After reading an early version of this manuscript a friend commented, "This book is like condensed milk—a rich concentration

3

of wisdom with a diversity of applications." I certainly hope you find that to be true, especially the diversity of application.

My goal is to give skills and tools to individuals who are engaged in an entrepreneurial pursuit—**on a limited budget**. You possess the connectors to apply the contents of this book to the specifics of your life.

Who will benefit the most from this book? Those who are in the "early-to-mid-stages" of ramping up a new business. It's like eating chicken. Eat the meat and throw away the bones. And if you hit a bone, something that doesn't quite fit your situation, keep chewing around the bone. Perhaps there will be some meat on the other side. Business professionals considering whether or not this book is relevant, may want to listen to seasoned veteran Les Brown, ". . . [this book] will change the way I will do business."

If you implement just a few ideas from this book, you should be able to add at least $10,000 to your bank account within six months.

I can't guarantee what I just stated, because I do not know your credibility. I don't know your telephone skills. I know nothing about the way you present yourself to others. I don't know your work ethic or if your word is your bond. That's on your shoulders. Wear it well.

Regardless your passion, a startup business is kind of like building an addition on your home:

    A.  It's messier than previously anticipated.

    B.  It takes longer than previously anticipated.

    C.  It's more expensive than previously anticipated.

What you are reading on these pages has been formed in the crucible of painful experiences. And it works. But not without a few failures along the way. Truth be told, I have learned more from my failures than from my successes. I am writing this very honest and open book as a wounded healer—providing some skills, tools, and creative ideas for charting a course through the dense fog.

I will not waste your time, keeping the "fluff factor" down to 1.75 percent. Each chapter is to-the-point. No bull. No hype.

It is my hope that you hear the enthusiasm in my words. We generally hear/read the words, but it's the "music" that really captures us. I trust that you hear the music, the passion, as you make your way to the back cover. Most of all I hope that this is a fun read for you.

Let's look at all this in terms of mixing colors. If *Creative Vision* is yellow and *Practical Application* is blue—we're looking for green.

Everybody loves green. It transcends ethnicity, gender, religion, generation, and class. An alternative, long-winded title to this book could be *If Nothing is Happening in Your Business Right Now, Mix Up Sumpin' Green*!

**EXECUTIVE CONCEPTS:** At the top of the Ballinskelligs Bay on the southwesterly edge of the peninsula in County Kerry, Ireland, there is a pub with a sign boasting, "IRELAND'S MOST FANTASTIC VIEW, FOG PERMITTING." Even though before you is one of the most panoramic views to behold (view the image at CreateTheDemand. com), the elements involved in creating the weather seem to conspire together, keeping tourists from getting a clear view of the beautiful sight. Hence the brisk sale of scenic postcards.

What's my point? The presence of "fog" doesn't nullify the existence of the entrepreneurial vision you know is real. Take a mental picture of the vision you have developed for your business. Keep that mental snapshot clear in your mind's eye, kind of like a panoramic postcard image. Don't doubt in the fog what you know you "saw" on a clear day. Like Mark Twain said, "You can't depend upon your judgment when your imagination is out of focus."

Expect the fog to come in. Plan for it and use it to your advantage as an opportunity for internal growth. Personal character and perseverance are built when the fog comes in, not when the view is clear. Starting and developing a new business is important, but even more meaningful is who you become in the process.

It may sound corny, but work with me on this. Like the above-mentioned pub in Ireland, remind yourself and others about the panoramic vision of your business by placing a small sticky note above your computer screen, "(*NAME OF YOUR BUSINESS*)—A MOST FANTASTIC VIEW, FOG PERMITTING." If it makes you feel any better, I just looked up a few moments ago and saw the sticky note above my computer screen, designed to remind me of this section. See, we're bonding already! Before we get through this book together, we'll be getting along famously. . . .

**VISION RICH, CASH POOR:** Something that has been an important part of my life is the "Hot Potato Principle." We can call it the "HPP." Procrastination is its major enemy. It doesn't cost a penny to implement the HPP. What do I mean by this? Whatever is your responsibility in getting something accomplished, get it out of your hands as soon as possible. It could be sending your financial information to your accountant so that he or she can get your taxes done in a timely manner. It could be finishing a proposal so that a committee can determine whether or not to hire you. It could be the setting up a time and date for a conference call. Whatever it is, treat it like a hot potato. Get it out of your hands as quickly as possible. If there is a bottleneck, it's *not* going to be you. That's the Hot Potato Principle. Live by this principle and you will be viewed by others as a genuine can-do and will-do person. This is a major part of being a man or woman of integrity. People do not respond to your intentions. They respond to your behavior. When you say you are going to do something, do it . . . as soon as possible.

## Connecting the Dots:

- NGEclubs.com—Next Generation Entrepreneur Clubs (NGEC): Connecting Now With Later. A workbook resource that connects the contents of this book to the lives of young adults (15–26 years of age). The workbook is a comprehensive amount of engaging contents. The website is developed especially for NGEC leaders, with a guide for establishing an NGEC in your school or community. There is also a way for leaders to communicate helpful ideas that are working in their clubs. The workbook/book/audio book combination can be an effective tool for helping to develop purpose for our next generation through the entrepreneurial gateway. The understanding of future business plans tends to positively impact our present decisions and priorities.

- MyGreatPersonality.com—I heard once that 15 percent of business and career success has to do with technical competence, while 85 percent is due to one's interpersonal skills. I believe this statement. If it is true, it is very important to spend the time to understand the way you are wired behaviorally. This is a great website, giving a couple of options for you to determine your personality style. Do you want a quick "Snapshot" or do you want the more comprehensive "Photo Album" of yourself? It's your choice. Understanding the strengths and vulnerabilities of your personality is critical when trying to grasp how you deal with the ups and downs of relationships and also becoming more aware of the way you approach your entrepreneurial pursuit. An entire Entrepreneur Club may want to get the more comprehensive analysis of individual personality styles—the complete "Photo Album." One of the first Club meetings can be dedicated to discussing the interplay between business success and one's personality style.

## Entrepreneur Club Option: For Personal Reflection and/or Group Discussion

1.  What is the vision and mission of your business? Write everything down, getting an even clearer image of the panoramic view before you.

2.  Describe and define the fog as it relates to your entrepreneurial pursuit. In other words, what makes you confused and perplexed, unclear about the next step(s) as you attempt to implement your vision and mission?

3.  Joseph Conrad once stated, "It is not the clear-sighted who rule the world. Great achievements are accomplished in a blessed, warm fog." I suspect that no one reading this book is actually trying to rule the world, but what is your perspective on what this famous author is communicating, within the context of the theme of this book?

4.  What are some advancing-through-the-fog strategies that can lead to "great achievements" when (not if) the thick fog settles in around you and your business pursuit? With pen in hand, identify specific practical concepts you can implement, addressing five layers. List at least three tactics per layer. Let's officially call it the "*FERMS Fog Strategy*" (say that fast five times): i. **F**inancial, ii. **E**motional, iii. **R**elational, iv. **M**ental, v. **S**piritual

As you embark upon this reading experience, what are you hoping to receive from this book? Make a list of your expectations and check it when you are finished to see if I hit the bulls-eye for you. Grab a cup of coffee, kick off your shoes, and let's move on to the next chapter together, with your Internet-capable computer close by.

# CHAPTER TWO

# DINNER AND A BOOK

*If at first you don't succeed, skydiving is not for you.*

Francis Roberts

Verbal snapshot. I am in an Italian restaurant munching on some Chicken Alfredo, sitting across from two people my wife and I have known for years. We are reminiscing about old times.

The conversation dies down for a moment. I look across the table, with my fork midway between the plate and my mouth, and ask, "So, Lauretta, what are your plans for the future?"

She lifted her head with a surprised look. "What do you mean?"

"Oh, I don't know. Your daughters are all grown up, and you are ready for a new chapter in your life. I'm wondering how you want to fill that new chapter."

"I'm not sure," she stammered. "I really haven't given it much thought."

Lauretta has a unique gift from God. If it were possible to shatter a crystal goblet with a high note, this woman could do it.

Classically trained, she has traveled extensively throughout various parts of the world participating in operatic performances. She has taught in prestigious schools such as Duke Ellington School of Music, Baltimore School for the Arts, and Peabody.

In spite of all the successes, she has been handed some very difficult situations. A widow with three lovely grown daughters, Lauretta has confronted much personal heartache and a number of vocational obstacles. She is a survivor.

## The Concept

Throughout the next twenty-five to thirty minutes, I laid out a practical action plan for her to start a new one-woman show specifically built around her training and her passion.

Here's the concept in a nutshell: An African American woman, Lauretta will perform some of the old Negro Spirituals at corporate functions, conventions, and Black History events for government agencies, churches, educational institutions, and family reunions. These performances will be both educational and inspirational. The organizations that hire her will be blown away by the experience. In fact, I can see her being sponsored by a large corporation to do this all over the world.

Can you see it? The lights will dim. She will turn her back to the audience, putting on vintage clothing. A hat. A shawl. Transformation. When she turns around, the single spotlight hits her. She will become Harriet Tubman, Phillis Wheatley, Sojourner Truth, or Minnie Tate, one of the original Fisk University Jubilee Singers. After dramatically providing the historical backdrop she will sing a song that will chill you down to the marrow of your bones.

After a short pause I added, "What you just heard is about $10,000 worth of advice. And I am willing to help you implement every step." I could see the excitement dancing in her eyes.

While driving home from the restaurant, I began to think about the many people who reach out to me for business and marketing advice. When could I carve out the time to place this information in written form so that others could benefit? The book you now hold in your hands is the result.

In fact, I want to write in such a way that you will almost feel like you are sitting at the next table, eavesdropping on what I told Lauretta. Perhaps you can glean some basic information for your own entrepreneurial pursuits. I sure hope so.

Let's see, weren't you the one who ordered the chicken pasta? There ain't no bones in that dish! Pretend you're not listening, but scoot your chair over a bit closer and tilt your head just a little to the right. . . .

---

**EXECUTIVE CONCEPTS:** Eulogize the mundane things of life. Do not overlook the obvious. A simple dinner conversation became the seed concept for a book. This book. What is the "normal stuff" in your life that can spark a new idea? Frankly, this book will free up my time, allowing me to become more productive. I generously give hours every month helping people who have specific questions about building their personal entrepreneurial dreams. This book will permit me to do other things. *How?* Whenever someone calls or emails for business advice, I will gently suggest that he or she should first read this book. I can then say goodbye and go back to what I was doing before the phone rang or the email was answered. If, after reading the book, the caller still has unanswered questions I will gladly resume the conversation. This strategy will help me superintend and multiply my time, while still helping people, which is very important to me.

**VISION RICH, CASH POOR:** Learn a new language. Assuming that you speak English *pretty good,* you may want to consider learning Spanish, Chinese, French, or Portuguese. It will give you access to many more people and will also expand your future business options. Regardless of where you live in the world, take a look at the changing demographics in your areas; along with the populations that will be expanding in the next twenty years and personally plan for the cultural realities of the future. Your future.

## Connecting the Dots:

- LanguageCrazy.com—Want to learn a new language? Want proven results? Here is a great place to start.

- LaurettaYoung.com—Lauretta is a real person. Check out her ever-expanding website and cheer her on with an encouraging email. Who knows? You may even have an idea or two for her as she is embarking upon this new chapter in her life.

## Entrepreneur Club Option:
## For Personal Reflection and/or Group Discussion

1. In what ways is your counsel in demand? Identify those categories, writing them down on paper. How much time do you spend per month freely helping people in each category?

2. What are the ways you can free up yourself so that you can remain focused on the entrepreneurial things about which you are passionate—and still help people?

3. "Of those who fail, most fail not realizing how close they were to success." I don't know the author, but what does that statement mean to you? Any personal stories or experiences that you know of that can illustrate this quotation?

# CHAPTER THREE

# DEATH OF A VISION

*What could be worse than being born without sight?*
*Being born with sight and no vision.*

Helen Keller

*What doesn't kill me only makes me stronger.*

Anonymous

A child is conceived in ecstasy but birthed with much pain.

Isn't that the way it is with life? Ideas and dreams tumble into our consciousness with great enthusiasm and passion, but the implementation of those concepts invites suffering and pain.

We all desire character traits like stick-to-itiveness, flexibility, generosity, perseverance, and integrity. We want to say what we mean and mean what we say. Giving birth to an entrepreneurial dream will test the very seams of your soul.

## Five Stages of a Business Vision

I can't remember where I heard it, but there are five stages of the growth of a vision. (I've embellished them a bit.)

1. **D**ream (exhilaration, excitement, skyrockets at night . . .)

2. **D**iscover overall purpose of vision (big picture thinking, finding a mentor . . .)

3. **D**evelop strategic aspects of vision (business plan, financing, equipment, technology, connecting with people who can help . . .)

4. **D**elegate (systems, protocol, insurance, retirement plans, employees . . .)

5. **D**isappear (backing off, letting others fail and/or succeed on their own, succession . . .)

Whoever came up with these stages knew what he or she was talking about. By the way, it is the non-participants who generally get the credit in the end. But if you don't care who gets the credit, do the details with dignity and integrity. After thinking carefully about this, I'd like to add another stage:

6. **D**eath of the vision. (disillusionment, wanting to quit, more questions than answers . . . )

I'm not sure where this category appears in the stages mentioned above, but it's a necessary part of the overall purpose of the vision. Here's the fun part. Sometimes the "death" stage visits a few times during the growth process.

Death of a vision comes in various forms, from without and from within: personal attack from a friend or unethical behavior from a trusted business partner that rips the guts out of your enthusiasm for the business and makes your creative juices congeal.

A sudden, unexpected downturn in the economy that directly impacts your business.

It's a period when you are working crazy hours and nothing seems to be happening. The bills are piling up and there doesn't seem to be any light at the end of the tunnel. It's hard for you to stop, rethink what you are doing, and figure out why you started doing it in the first place.

Why? Because you have invested so much financial and emotional capital in your venture and it's difficult to take a rest and evaluate everything.

The fear of failure can paralyze one person, immobilizing him or her—resulting in reduced creativity or productivity. *What if this doesn't work?* Or that same fear can send another person hurtling down the entrepreneurial autobahn at 150 mph. *The loster I am, the faster I go.*

Call it what you like. Dry times. Emptiness. Desert experience. Famine. Savoring the goodness and excitement of life is tantamount to chewing shredded cardboard. It can slowly change a happy-go-lucky visionary into a cold, calculating cynic.

## Three Questions

One may start asking questions:

1. Who am I? (Strikes at the core of one's *identity*.)
2. Why am I here? (Strikes at the core of one's *significance* and *purpose*.)
3. Where am I going? (Strikes at the core of one's *destiny*.)

These three questions must be answered. But the answers seem so far away. I don't want to over-dramatize this, but an entrepreneurial pursuit will challenge you and the ones who love you like nothing else you have ever attempted.

What compelled people such as Thomas Edison, George Washington Carver, Martin Luther, Mother Teresa, Martin Luther King, Mary McLeod Bethune, Charles Wesley, Joan of Arc, William Wilberforce, and so many others to achieve great things? Why do some people completely commit to a vision, regardless of the cost? What kind of a personal epiphany does a common, ordinary person experience at such times?

## The Popeye Moment

Bill Hybels' response is that these people reach a point of absolute discontent with the way things are. He calls it the *Popeye Moment*: "I've stood all I can stands and I can't stands it no more."

Death of a vision may be the catalyst that causes some to experience a Popeye Moment. In *The Screwtape Letters*, C.S. Lewis puts it this way, "All horrors have followed the same course, getting worse and forcing you into a kind of bottleneck till, at the very moment when you thought you must be crushed, behold! You were out of the narrows and all was suddenly well. The extraction hurt more and more and then the tooth was out. The dream became a nightmare and then you awoke. You die and die and then you are beyond death."

## A Personal Story

Each one of us has our Popeye story. If you don't, you will. Allow me to share a bit of my story. In 1993 I stepped away from a vocation I had enjoyed for eighteen years. I knew it was time for a change, but I wasn't sure what was on the other side of that transition.

Up to this point a lot of resumé/obituary-type stuff had happened in my life: mentor/chaplain for the NBA Washington Bullets/Wizards for nineteen years (1979–1998); radio talk show host for eleven years; TV show host for six years; author of a few international bestselling books.

I won't go into detail, but I found myself in a blue funk with more questions than answers. In fact, one of my books, *When Life Isn't Fair: Making Sense Out of Suffering*, is the culmination of wisdom lessons learned prior to and during this period. I went through the death of a vision, some of it is far too personal to include in any book.

I knew that in a period of personal transition the world wasn't going to stop. The gas and electric, automobile, insurance, and mortgage companies weren't going to give me a break on my payments. Because I'm not really good at sitting around twiddling my thumbs waiting for things to happen, I needed to crank the economic engine and keep the money flowing in. But how? Why? And where was I going to earn the money to keep my head above water?

Driven by the need to pay the bills, I started exploring a few business endeavors. I got involved in ventures that were way out of my arenas of expertise or passion. I was grasping at straws.

One such enterprise was a 35,000 square foot indoor flea market that operated only on weekends. I discovered late in the game that not everything with the business partnership was as I had originally thought. A lot of money flowed in initially, but the venture soon failed for a myriad of reasons ranging from poor public relations to "creative" behind-the-scenes book keeping. It seemed like a blind alley. A waste of time and energy.

I went into network marketing with a company that was promising to come out with a new "gee-whiz" consumer electronics product every month. I had never gotten involved in network marketing before this venture. While I was intrigued by the concept, the timing had never been right. I was always busy with another vocation, and there had never been a product line that had captured my attention. But now I decided to check it out. I was able to build a rather large organization. It was an exciting, educational, and quite successful ride in the first year. But soon the company wasn't able to deliver on the new products in a timely manner and everything fizzled out. Another dead end street.

I learned a lot from these and other ventures, but I was still in a quandary. I wondered: What is my purpose in this new chapter of my life? What do I do the best? What am I going to do when I grow up?

## How The Freeman Institute® Started

Bill Kissinger, a friend of mine who is a successful financial planner, asked me to facilitate a teambuilding workshop for his employees. I had never facilitated a professional seminar for a company before; but I consented, and we set a date. He gave me an overview of what he wanted to accomplish in the team building session, and I started developing an agenda for the day-long training. At the appointed time his nine employees and I gathered in their conference room and we had a productive, enjoyable time. I didn't know what to charge him. I think he gave me five hundred dollars for my services. All I know is that I was thrilled. "Five hundred bucks for a day's work? You've got to be kidding! Where do I sign up for a gig like this?"

A month or so later Bill called me. "I want you to know that the employees haven't stopped talking about your seminar. They loved the experience, and it has actually changed the way we communicate with each other. Joel, we have known each other for a number of years and I am aware that you have been casting about, searching for your next career. I think that you ought to consider doing staff development and leadership seminars."

I didn't quite know what to say. Speechlessness doesn't happen to me very often. I finally responded with a "thank you" and some questions about the logistics of starting out as a professional speaker. He said that he would write a reference letter (which I still have) and he would also open up his Rolodex, giving me the names and contact information of some of his best clients.

What was I going to do? What a picture! A slender, thirty-nine-year-old guy in a bit of a funk emotionally, not even knowing what questions to ask. I was talented in some ways and educated, but I had no mentor to help develop a specific business plan; no idea about what to charge for a day of training; and no money to get this thing jump-started. And I'm going to develop a professional speaking/corporate training business that is supposed to motivate and encourage others? You've got to be kidding! I was so low that I was almost to the point of licking the dust off a sidewalk.

This was the start of The Freeman Institute®. My vision? *To provide world-class staff development and leadership programs to people in organizations around the globe.* Around the world? No way! I hardly had enough money or momentum to take a walk around the block! It was 1994, and I didn't have a clue what I was getting myself into and the personal growth I would encounter. Plus, I had no awareness of the level of difficulty in starting a seminar/professional speaking business from scratch.

There are a number of metaphors I could use: rising like a phoenix from the ashes; death, burial, and resurrection.

I was about to embark upon a vision that would die a few deaths. By the way, every seasoned entrepreneur has at least one death-of-a-vision story. What's your story, along with the wisdom lessons you have learned? I'd like to hear of your adventures.

---

**EXECUTIVE CONCEPTS:** I have a profound respect for people who are fighting alcohol or drug addiction—addictions of any kind. Why? Because when I look into their eyes, I am looking deeply into the soul of someone who has had to confront self-centeredness, self-ishness, self-justification, juvenile thinking, and juvenile behavior like few other people on the planet.

There are similar dynamics with entrepreneurs. You will accomplish much, but that is not the primary focus. The real issue is what and who you will become in the process. You will confront laziness, excuses, rationalization, and stupid thinking along the way. The biggest enemy is not the IRS; it's not your competition; it's not the negativity from your own family or other external factors. The biggest enemy is you. Your own stuff. The things that hook you. Your own issues that you have brought with you from childhood.

Create a "eulogy list" of your past business successes and failures. Make a copy and then symbolically bury that copy to ceremoniously give yourself a fresh start. (Perhaps take the list, burn it, sending the ashes into the wind, or wad up the list and say, "Thank you, God!" then flush it all away.) The idea is to set yourself free from your past to be able to step into your new future today! Hold on to the original to help you remember the date of this milestone in your life. It will also come in handy when writing your autobiography.

In many ways, embarking upon an entrepreneurial pursuit will test you like nothing else you have ever done. Relatively speaking, very few people can handle being an entrepreneur. The challenges range from lack of discipline and pure laziness to fear of rejection, terrible work ethic, trying to do the work of four people, lack of follow-through and lack of funds. The mere fact that you have gotten this far shows me that you just might be made of the right stuff.

**VISION RICH, CASH POOR:** Are you making a lot of international telephone calls? There are a few companies springing up that utilize web-based technology, allowing you to make calls anywhere in the world over the Internet. Almost free. The voice quality is improving all the time.

**BONUS:** Talking about making international phone calls reminds me of something else—telephone answering systems. When first starting out, you will want to make your business office appear as big as possible to your potential clients. A sophisticated telephone answering system is the key. TalkSwitch is one of the finest systems that not only performs flawlessly, but also is quite inexpensive. I own one and I am thrilled with it! Check them out at TalkSwitch.com

## Connecting the Dots:

- Skype.com—At the moment it is one of the more popular Internet-based companies for international phone calls, including free video calls. By the time you read this, there may be others providing healthy competition. Research and then dive into this wonderful technology.

- WhenYourVisionDies.com—If you are the founder or one of the founders of a successful entrepreneurial business and have connected with this chapter, I would like to talk with you. I am writing a new book, expanding on this theme. Go to the website and follow the protocol. Perhaps you would like to be interviewed for this new book project.

## Entrepreneur Club Option:
## For Personal Reflection and/or Group Discussions

1. What drives you, truly motivates you—beyond a paycheck?

2. What is your death-of-a-vision story? Have you ever written it down? As mentioned above, I'd like to hear experiences.

3. What wisdom lessons have you learned from that period in your life?

4. How are you passing those wisdom lessons on to the next generation?

# CHAPTER FOUR

# DESIGNING YOUR FUTURE

*Twenty years from now you will be more disappointed by the things you didn't do than by the ones you did. So throw off the bowlines. Sail away from the safe harbor. Catch the trade winds in your sails. Explore. Dream.*

Mark Twain

Let's take a step back to the second chapter where I introduced Lauretta. As a technically-challenged person, she had a look of quasi-terror in her eyes when I mentioned the first phase of her new endeavor.

"Lauretta, first things first. You need to provide the information required to create a website with a few buttons. Executive Summary. Bio/Resumé. Testimonials. Repertoire. Photographs. Contact Information." Her response? Gulp.

Why a website?

1. In this day and age, if you don't have a website you're not really in business.

2. This is one of the more creative, productive, and less boring ways to do a strategic business plan—let's call

it a BPI (Business Plan Incognito). You will need to address the nitty gritty financial aspects of your business in due time, however the process required to develop a website will address most of the legitimate questions you need to answer before you can hit prime time with your venture (Who? What? Why? When? Where? How?).

3. Once you have addressed the major questions and developed content, you not only know the all-important answers to those questions, *but you now also have a website.* This is a huge accomplishment. The process you endured in the development of a website has forced you to understand what you are all about and how you are going to implement the vision that is burning within. In essence, you have now completed the public version of your business plan; your digital brochure.

Forget about making a regular paper brochure at the beginning stages of a business. Brochures are costly to develop, design, print, and mail. Plus nobody really reads them. Later on a professional brochure may be important, but at the first, it's not necessary. A website and a simple business card with your three main objectives printed on the back can take you far during the early days. The business card is designed to point people to your website.

I used to mail out promotional material to everyone who expressed interest. That got really expensive, with very little return on investment (R.O.I.) for all that had been mailed. But things have changed—for the good. I rarely, if ever, send out a "propaganda" packet in the mail. No videos. No DVDs. No brochures. It's all online. If Austin Powers were to weigh in on this topic, he would look at you out of the corner of his eyes with a wry grin and wink, "It's digital, Baby!"

When someone calls and asks for a packet of information to be mailed, here's my standard eco-conscious reply, "Let's not chop down another tree. Check out my website. It has generic course overviews for all of my seminar programs. The video clips of some of my presentations will give you a sense of my presentation style and audience response. Please give me your email address and I will send you my *digital propaganda letter* within the next ten minutes."

The person chuckles and then gives me his or her email address. I have yet to experience one objection to that approach. I may respond differently if I think that mailing one of my books or a DVD presentation will help the key-decision-makers make up their minds about utilizing my services. But that is rare.

## Gateways to Your Future

A website is like a huge building with many entrances. Develop entry portals that will attract some people who may never come directly to your site, but who enter through a portal that is not an essential aspect of your business.

Web surfers have their own reasons for visiting a website, with different results. Because of such a "chance" visit, your arenas of expertise will be reviewed by someone who may want to invite you to his or her next company event. Or your products will be purchased by another person who had never heard of you before. Or the serendipitous experience of visiting your site may be shared with the Web surfer's brother-in-law, who just so happens to be the key-decision-maker of another large organization needing your services. Sound confusing? It's not.

On my main website (FreemanInstitute.com) I have some of the following doorways:

- Ancient Egyptian Photo Gallery (230 photos and expanding)

- Around the World in 80 Clicks (web cams around the world)

- Pretty Funny Stuff (everything is good, clean fun and it has to make me laugh out loud)

- The Freeman Institute® Black History Collection (oldest piece, dated 1597)

- Hundreds of "not-your-typical" Quotable Quotes (you see some of them at the beginning of each chapter and in the Bonus Material)

- Online courses: Diversity, Conflict Resolution, and Workplace Violence

- 3-D images that require special glasses

- Family trips with photos (Showing how any parent can take his or her children anywhere in the world)

- A portal designed specifically for non-profit and faith-based organizations

- A portal designed specifically for military organizations

- Critical Incident Debriefing (Unique and highly special-ized ten-hour process for senior executives, other key em-ployees, professional athletes, and entertainers)

- Many other doorways . . .

Some may not agree with my philosophy of Web development, but here is my rationale: Many surf to my website looking for a quotation or humorous item for their next newsletter or speech. While checking out the information that drew them to enter one of my website doorways, they discover that I facilitate seminars and deliver keynote speeches. The individual then places this in an email folder or file. I get a call seven months later requesting my presence at their company's next convention. When I ask, I am told the story on how they heard about my services. I continue to be amazed.

Others may bump into my company website because of their interest in the ancient Egyptian photographs I have taken on my trips to Egypt and to museums around the world (Paris, London, Rome, Cairo, Philadelphia, Chicago, etc.). Soon they realize that I make Diversity and Black History presentations. I may get a call some months later requesting my presence at a Black History Month or Diversity Day event in Los Angeles, Miami, Detroit, Houston, or London.

From where did that call originate? From someone who came through one of my many portals. We would have never met otherwise.

Also, I sometimes give a pair of 3-D glasses at events. There may be two thousand in the audience, but only one person receives the special glasses, based upon his or her birthday or longest distance traveled. While I am briefly explaining the use of the glasses for that person, everyone in the audience is growing in their curiosity about wanting to visit the website to see what I am talking about. How many websites have 3-D pages? Not enough to make it a normal Internet experience.

If you are a small-business person, I encourage you to learn how to do your own website publishing. Keep looking until you find a website designer who will teach you the basics of web design.

Why? So glad you asked. Because most of the skilled people who maintain websites are so busy that your request will probably not be fulfilled for two to three weeks and you will be charged a premium rate. And once the changes have been made, you will be frustrated, because it wasn't quite what you wanted. You are then left to wait another few days for the corrections to be made.

## Becoming Computer-Friendly

Back in the 1990s, I was proud of the fact that I was so computer illiterate that I did not even know how to turn off a computer. I had written all my books by hand and refused to bow my knee to the use of computers. I considered fooling around with computers a classic waste of my time. I was above all that.

That same year I was in Barbados doing some leadership training for the permanent secretaries of the government. I met Errol Griffith who worked for the Ministry of Tourism. We became fast friends. After getting to know each other better, my stand-offish view of computers was revealed. He gently challenged me to become familiar with computers. I chuckled and said, "Naw, I am doing very well without those things, thank you very much."

A while later I was "taken to school" by Jeff Wright, a friend visiting from Chicago. We had a computer for the kids in the house, but I didn't mess with it. Jeff knew of my anti-computer attitude. After dinner Jeff suggested that he and I go into the computer room to check out the computer.

We sat down and he asked me to think of a topic, an event or a person. Immediately I said, "Washington Bullets." He then told me to enter that term in a search engine. I was amazed! So much information came up that I hardly knew where to start. We sat together in front of the computer well into the night. Four hours later, I was hooked. I knew that I would have to learn about computers.

I decided to take six months to ramp up my knowledge of computers and the Internet. My children were a huge help. Latrent

Smith, a gentleman who lived across the street from us, was a web designer for a government agency Intranet site. He consented to help me understand web design. I knew that this was going to transform my entire business model.

For a nominal fee Latrent created a unique template that reflected the image I wanted to project. He loaded a basic web design program (FrontPage) on my computer, and he showed me how to use it and was available to answer some of my questions.

There are other web design programs, like Dreamweaver. There are also some web-based design programs that are absolutely goof-proof. With web-based software there are hundreds of templates from which to choose and within two to three days you can personally create a workable website that communicates exactly what you want to convey to your potential clients. Plus you get to update the content and photos any time of the day or night.

Back to Latrent. I asked him to do the initial website template and leave the grunt work to me. Slowly but surely I learned how to create web pages. I also learned about the maintenance aspects. Here I was—someone who formerly had zero knowledge about the Internet; now I had enough knowledge and experience to be "dangerous."

Guess what. I now do all my own web work, with over five hundred pages of material on my main website. I'm not bragging or complaining. Occasionally I have to call my oldest son, David, for help, but for the most part I am quite independent.

There are days I will update my website five to six times. A thought will strike me, and I will immediately make the changes and republish those pages until it reflects the way I want it to look. Within seconds anyone bumping into my website from anywhere in the world is getting the latest information I want to communicate. It is very liberating to not have to be dependent upon someone else to update my website any time I want to make a change.

## *Seven* Commandments

Here is my philosophy about the design and maintenance of a website (Ten Commandments seemed . . . well . . . a bit ostentatious):

1. The website needs to be professional, but not so professional that it looks and feels clinical and cold—unless that's the image you want to portray. I prefer a look and feel that makes a person want to get a cup of coffee, kick off his or her shoes for a while, and enjoy the experience. I also want my website to be the topic of conversation around the office during lunch. "I encountered a rather crazy website this morning. There is a section called *Pretty Funny Stuff* that almost made me fall off my seat with laughter. You gotta see it. And the guy does some seminar about people who drive you crazy. We should get him to come here. . . ."

2. Keep the web pages clean and simple. Stay away from a lot of graphics, and stay away from flash technology. It looks cool, but you have to be concerned about the time it takes for a page to load. Think about your own attention span while surfing the Internet. After three to five seconds, waiting for a page to load, many people are gone—never to return.

3. Make sure that images are cropped and resized to the exact size you want on your web page. Many will use a huge image and then will make it appear smaller on the

web page itself. This will create an inordinately long period of time for the page to load, because the image file is still huge.

4. Create a site map. People need to be able to wrap their arms around the basic themes of your site, especially if you have over five hundred pages of content. Make it easy to navigate, with easy-to-read buttons located in an easy-to-find spot on each page.

5. Do not make the surfer scroll right. Scrolling down is okay, but it might be better to place a small amount of content on one page so that people do not have to scroll down too much.

6. Keep your links updated. Within the context of our topic, there are few things worse than clicking on a hyperlink that brings an interested person to a blank page.

7. Provide enough information to keep people wanting more. For example, if you are selling a book, include the first chapter so that a potential customer will get a taste of your writing style and content. Leave them wanting more. Provide some other educational aspects that inform and entertain.

This ain't brain surgery. What are your pet peeves as you surf the Internet? Pop-up ads? Banner ads? Splash pages? Background wallpaper that distracts from the content? Pages that take too long to load? Frames? Font size too small or too large? Too much content? Too little content? Cold, clinical feel? Stay away from anything that drives you nuts. A lot of this is common sense. But common sense isn't always common practice. By the way, animated images that dance about, wink, and exhibit intriguing moves are generally cheesy and ultimately distract from your content.

# Digital Real Estate

Purchase every dot-com domain name that relates somehow to your business. This is digital real estate. For the most part people naturally think that a domain name ends with a "dot com." Stay away from the "dot biz," "dot tv," "dot net," and other URL endings. Use the "dot org" only if you have a non-profit organization. And then purchase the "dot com" version. That way if people looking for information type the "dot com" by mistake, they still reach you.

With free forwarding and masking you can use each domain name for its own purpose. At this moment I own well over 200 domain names and counting—from one of the best and least expensive places: MultiWebConcepts.com. Each domain name is forwarded to a specific page on the FreemanInstitute.com website and then masked to make it look like it is its own website. I am paying for only one website, but it looks like The Freeman Institute® has many websites. This makes it practical, economical, and expansive.

If you want to get a sneak peak into the future plans of The Freeman Institute®, take a look at my current domain names. Of course, none of the future-plan domain names are mentioned in this book. I always stake out my digital real estate claim and establish it on several levels before I breathe a word about my idea to another soul.

Below is a sampling of the domain names to give you some ideas. Check out a few of them at random to see where they take you:

> FreemanInstitute.com, GreatWorkshops.com, Freemani.com,
> AngerSeminar.com, greatEseminars.com, Black101.com,
> DiversitySeminar.com,DiversitySeminars.com,AstoundingImage.com,
> JohariGame.com, BlackHistoryPostcards.com, FreemanStuff.com,

BlackGlory.com, BlackHistoryCards.com, CIDcoach.com,
WhiteMansJourney.com,360wisdom.com,iHateBoringSeminars.com,
DiversityIsGood.com,DiversityThatWorks.com,DiversityCrazy.com,
CrazyWorkshop.com, CrazyWorkshops.com, CrazySeminar.com,
CrazySeminars.com, CrazyRadioSeminar.com, ChurchCrazy.com,
CrazyRadioSeminars.com,BoringWorkshops.com,BlackThink.com,
DealingWithPeopleWhoDriveYouCrazy.com,GreatWorkshops.com,
JoelWritesRealGood.com, JoelSpeaksRealGood.com,
TruthCentric.com, Truth-Centric.com, TheMomentBook.com,
SmokeEscapeHood.com, SmokeEscapeHoods.com,
TripsWithDad.com, SphinxOfGiza.com, FeedbackCoach.com,
DeathToADream.com,DeathToAVision.com,WhenYourDreamDies.com,
WhenYourVisionDies.com, ItTakesACity.org, ItTakesACity.com,
ItTakesATown.com, ItTakesASchool.com, ItTakesACollege.com,
ItTakesAUniversity.com,ItTakesACountry.com,ItTakesAChurch.com,
ItTakesACompany.com, VisionRichCashPoor.com,
LeadershipCrazy.com, TheFreemanEnterprises.com,
FreemanInstituteFoundation.org, NGEclubs.com,
WorkHardWorkSmart.com, WHWS.mobi. . .

Yup, you guessed it; I own both IfNobodyLovesYou.com *and* CreateTheDemand.com.

Let's say I am being interviewed on a radio talk show in Atlanta. The host and I are having a great time discussing the diversity seminar program that I developed. The host then asks me to mention my website. It's confusing to send the listeners to FreemanInstitute.com and then tell them to look on the left-hand side of the screen, clicking on the ninth button down from the top.

I can hear a confused listener driving in traffic talking to his radio, "How do you spell it? Is that freedman, friedman, freimann, or freeman? And what was that again . . . the ninth button down on the left hand side of the second screen?"

Someone driving in city traffic isn't going to remember all that. The domain name DiversitySeminars.com is easy to remember and it takes them to the right page on my website. And I also own the alternate "singular-case" version, DiversitySeminar.com, just in case someone didn't hear it quite right.

Pick domain names that are easy to remember. Any time you have to explain the spelling you have already lost the attention of most people. Stay away from purchasing any domain names that elicit furrowed brows, quizzical looks, and crinkled noses. When people ask me for my company website I will generally tell them to go to GreatWorkshops.com. It's quick, simple, and easy to remember. Plus it immediately communicates what I do.

## "DotMobi" and Your Future

It won't be long before we will be able to say that well over a billion people connect to the Internet through their mobile phones. In fact, by the time you read this, it may already be true. Already countries like Japan, South Korea, and Finland are way ahead of North America by the way they utilize wireless, broadband, and mobile technology for the benefit of the masses. How will you and your website content respond to the international movement toward online connection through mobile/cellular technology?

DotMobi is the first and only top level domain dedicated to delivering the Internet to mobile/cell phones. DotMobi is revolutionizing the use of the Internet. It is designed to guide mobile users to made-for-mobile Internet content and services that can be accessed with confidence.

DotMobi domain names became available for the general public in late 2006. Since that time, tens of thousands of dotMobi domain names have been sold. DotMobi sites solve the biggest barriers to mobile Internet use—poorly formatted pages, inappropriate or excessive content, difficult logins, difficult navigation, and slow access and long load times, leading to costly mobile bills.

As you protect your brand in the dotMobi world, make sure that you purchase domain names with the least number of characters possible. MultiWebConcepts.com has a search engine designed to help you determine what is and what is not available with dotMobi and other international domain names. Be creative. If a domain name you want has already been taken, add the word "my" in front of it or something like "101" or "123" at the end of it. It's all thumbs when using a mobile phone to type in a domain name, so make it as short and user friendly as possible.

I own a number of dotMobi domain names, like WHWS.mobi (WorkHardWorkSmart), where you can download a free mp3 file with sample chapters from the audio book version of this book. Instead of showing you too many of my own dotMobi websites, allow me to give a couple of famous examples that will illustrate the look and feel of a dotMobi website. Take a look at NBA.mobi, AAA.mobi and BMW.mobi to see how their websites are optimized for viewing on a mobile phone. It's a minimalist's paradise. Less is more. While you build your dotMobi empire, continue to expand your thinking as the planet shrinks. Stay ahead of the curve. This is your present and future digital reality. Design it well.

## The Business Benefits of Web Blogging

*Blog* is short for *web log*. It's an Internet site or sub-site where a person or organization can post usually brief bits of text, along with relevant links to other sites with more text, photos, audio and/or video. There are all kinds of blogs: news, educational, political, religious, sports, hobbies, cultural—you name it. Personal blogs are all over the Internet with opinions as varied as the hues and tones of the color spectrum.

Remember the run-up to the American 2004 elections when the top political bloggers were invited to attend both the Republican and Democratic conventions as members of the press? This was the first time I can remember that blogging had made the front page of our local newspaper. And it's becoming more and more mainstream. But what about blogging and your business?

Blogs aren't for everybody. But unlike other ideas that went nuts during the dot-com bubble, they are becoming a big deal, especially when it comes to improving communication with customers. Who is the primary blogging audience? It's the young, affluent, broadband-connected male. If that is part of your audience, you may need to take note.

Two books help to give an overview for you:

1. *Blogwild!* by Andy Wibbels (Portfolio, 175 pages). Wibbels has good insights and useful experiences, and is an easy-to-read writer.

2. *Naked Conversations* by Robert Scoble and Shel Israel (Wiley, 251 pages). Some of the most enlightening parts of this book are the examples of how not to blog.

Not every entrepreneurial pursuit will benefit from this intriguing medium, but you won't know until you learn more, and reading these books is a smart way to embark upon your journey into the world of blogging.

There are many benefits to blogging, ranging from boosting your website's search engine rankings, great customer newsletters, getting instant feedback to ideas, and providing a sense of community to networking for your career, staying fresh in the minds of your customers, a low-cost way to enhance your website, and positioning yourself as an expert.

The bottom line is that bloggers are generally better-informed than non-bloggers. Knowing more is a career advantage.

I have some other Internet ideas that I use every day. But you didn't think that I was going to tell you all of my secrets in this book, did you?

**EXECUTIVE CONCEPTS:** Let me take a few moments to speak to a certain, more chronologically mature audience. I know that you didn't grow up with computers like the younger generation(s). You may even suffer from a mild case of "computer phobia." Let me speak to you as one who grew up in a one-horse town in Alberta, Canada, with no television in our home. And as one who used to rush home after school to listen to the radio version of the *Green Hornet* or *Gunsmoke* on the Drumheller radio station, CJDV. Enough reminiscing. Here's what I wanted to say to you: Developing your own website is truly easier than it looks. Whatever price you pay to become more web-literate will deliver rich dividends to you for the rest of your life. Face it, the Internet is here to stay. The more you understand about web design, the more relevant your website will be to potential clients.

Here are at least three legitimate web design philosophies:

1. Hire someone else. Having a trusted friend do the web work frees you up to do what you do best.

2. Attend a daylong seminar so that you know enough to ask the right questions of your web designer and make intelligent suggestions.

3. Find someone who will mentor you. Understand the mechanics of web design and start doing the basic maintenance work and updates yourself. Your entire website can be on your laptop. I have updated my website while traveling on the plane, publishing the changes later that evening in the hotel room through their wireless connection.

The first option can become frustrating to you. Because, as we mentioned before, most web designers are extremely busy. I lean toward a combination of the second and third options. In my opinion, the look and feel of your website is something you cannot afford to delegate to someone else. Understand the mechanics of web design and start doing the basic maintenance work and updates yourself, after the basic template has been created by an expert.

**VISION RICH, CASH POOR:** If nobody loves your website, how can you create more of a demand? There's another way to put it. How much would you pay for a qualified lead? Three cents a lead? A nickel? A dime? A quarter? A great way to get your goods and/or services noticed is to bid on search terms that people would use to find you and your business. For instance, if you own rental property on the beach of a beautiful lake, put yourself in the place of a person trying to locate a three-bedroom home for a cost-effective family vacation. Bid on the terms you would use yourself to find such a property. Go to your favorite search engine, using the terms "pay per click" to see what comes up. Do your research. Locate the best "Pay-Per-Click" company. And then bid on the terms that will drive clients to your website. There are even websites that weigh the pros and cons of the various "Pay-Per-Click" companies out there. Caution. Monitor this very closely, or else the bills of your first few months will be out of sight! Once you get a handle on it, you will see activity on your website that wasn't there before.

It's an idea worth exploring. Just make sure that you bid only on search terms that will generate income for you. You don't want to bid on search terms that will ultimately attract a thousand middle school students to your website to help them with their research papers—unless you sell resources to the parents of middle school students writing research papers. You want the kind of traffic that makes your cash register ring. Get my drift?

**BONUS:** The Internet is the great equalizer. That's one of the things I love about it! It isn't hyper-conscious about race, gender, religion, age, or class—like some of the world is in everyday life. Age discrimination works at both ends of life. You can be a 14-year-old teenager developing 2-D games for cell phones in the privacy of your bedroom. As long as the games are excellent, no one knows or cares how young you are. In fact, once a few newspapers write stories about your business venture, investors will flock your way. Let's change the channel. Ex-offenders run into many employment challenges. You can be someone who has paid your debt to society, serving fourteen years in prison. As long as your products are what a lot of people want, you can make a decent living by selling items on auction websites like eBay. No one has to know about your past. No frowns. No judgments. My point? Take advantage of the anonymity the Internet provides, especially if you feel that you are experiencing any of the various types of discrimination in your everyday life.

## Connecting the Dots:

- MultiWebConcepts.com—This is a great place to purchase domain names and website hosting options that is incredibly inexpensive and easy to use. They also have goof-proof web-based software for creating your own website within a short period of time and with no prior knowledge of web design. With a standard registration, your name, address, postal and email addresses are listed in the public WHOIS directory. When you purchase a domain name, consider making your registration information private. This option costs a little bit more, but it will shield your personal information from public view.

## Entrepreneur Club Option:
## For Personal Reflection and/or Group Discussion

1. If you are resistant to the concepts outlined in this chapter, what are the excuses about web development ricocheting around in your brain right now? Make a list of those excuses.

2. How do you respond to each excuse?

3. If you already do your own web work, what is your philosophy about the design and maintenance of a website? How many web design commandments can you come up with? That, by the way, just might be the beginnings of a booklet you will publish.

4. Sit down for about an hour, writing on paper all of the domain names you would like to own—expanding your digital real estate holdings. Be creative, letting the ideas flow. At MultiWebConcepts.com there is a search engine, designed to determine if Website domain names you want have been taken or not. Go there with the domain names on your list and follow directions. You will soon become a digital real estate mogul.

# CHAPTER FIVE

# BRANDING YOURSELF

*Wherever you are . . . be there.*

Freemanism

Let's say you are sitting in the aisle seat of an airplane having a wonderful conversation with the person next to you. His name is Bert. You have been talking about what he does for a living.

You're on a quick puddle-jumper flight. Bert's occupation is so unusual and fascinating that before you know it the plane has landed and almost everyone is standing in the aisle waiting to leave. The half-hour flight passed by so quickly.

Just as the people in front of you are getting ready to exit the plane Bert asks, "So, what do you do?" It seems like an inconvenient and untimely question, but you have about ten seconds to respond. What do you say?

Let me put it another way. What will you say in ten seconds that might cause Bert or another passenger within earshot to chase you up the ramp, asking for more information about what you do?

It's important to have a response designed for different audiences and also for different periods of time allotted: thirty seconds, one minute, three minutes, five minutes, ten minutes, thirty minutes, forty-five minutes, and sixty minutes. Know when to be brief. Know when to ask questions. Know when to shut up and listen. Really listen. (God gave us two ears and one mouth. There's a parable there somewhere.)

Branding yourself isn't nearly as painful as it may sound. You must determine your main strength(s) and then you can develop a creative spin to that strength. For instance, my company brand is seven words *Dealing With People Who Drive You Crazy!*®. That statement brings a smile to another person's face. It's quick. No long explanation. It fits my semi-off-the-wall sense of humor and is aligned with my passion to help people. It's also my five second response to someone like Bert who asks me what I do.

The brand of a company is like a zebra galloping with a herd of horses. It looks like a horse and runs like a horse—even blending in with the rest of the herd—if someone is only focusing specifically at the activity of running. But the black and white stripes of the zebra cause it to visually stand out up close or from far away.

That's part of the purpose of a brand. There are plenty goods and services out there, but a five to seven word brand and unique business practices—backed up with excellent customer service— can cause what you are doing to be set apart as something unique in the midst of many others doing the same type of things.

It is my belief that each one needs a bit of "schtick." How about an example? Thousands of people fix computers. But what makes some computer experts stand out? They show up to the designated place at the appointed time in "high water" trousers, lab coats, with plastic pocket protectors,and the middle part of their thick glasses taped up with white tape. They are doing the same thing that other computer experts are doing. But their business plan includes self-effacing geek-like humor, which is both endearing and reassuring to so many of us who are immobilized when our computers break down. A winning combination—standing out, coupled with outstanding service. Zebras in a herd of horses.

I am intrigued with the power of a branding statement. Let me switch the channel. Let's say I am on the phone with the gatekeeper of an influential person. I have just been asked, "What shall I say is your purpose for wanting to talk with Dr. Jones?"

It's a cold call and I have just a few seconds to make a compelling case or I am about to get the standard brush-off. "I would like to present an overview of my training and staff development programs," I begin. "The most popular seminar program is *Dealing With People Who Drive You Crazy!*®." I pause for just a moment to gauge her response and then add, "But you probably have never had to deal with anyone like that around there, have you?" My mischievous grin telegraphs over the phone.

It's a rare response on the other end of the line. The normally business-like gatekeeper literally laughs out loud. "Boy, do we ever need that around here! Let me see if Dr. Jones is available." Those seven words have once again opened the door. (For all I know Dr. Jones might have been the very one who was driving her crazy!) That's just a quick example of the power of a brand.

## Protecting Your Brand

By the way, I love this brand enough to have had it registered with the US Patent and Trademark Office. I also spend a few minutes every five to six months, searching the Internet to see if anyone else is using it. If so, I write them a warm and friendly email educating them about my ownership of those seven words arranged in that order. There are teeth behind my smile. I then ask them to consider using another statement. I even offer to help them create another title for their seminar program. Thus far the few people I have written to have responded very positively. Protecting your brand is very important.

Let me communicate a quick example about what happened on the evening of September 25 at around eight o'clock, just weeks before this book was completed: I did one of my routine searches on the Internet to see if anyone else was using the statement, *Dealing With People Who Drive You Crazy!®*. To my great surprise, I found a reputable publisher and wonderful author with a new book sporting the exact title—word-for-word! I was flabbergasted. How was I going to respond? The book cover was done, with an advertised February 2007 release date, approximately 5 months away. And it had already been listed with Amazon.com under that title, along with the image of the book cover!

I was shocked because most publishers research this kind of stuff before it even gets out of committee. The legal reality in the United States is that no book title can be copyrighted, but the marketing reality is that publishers do not want their titles to be confused with any other book. It makes business sense.

This seven-word statement is not only the title of my most popular seminar, but it also is the brand for my company. Plus, I have been working on a book with the same title.

Long story, short. I wrote a gentle and informative, but firm, email to the author and also to the chief editor of the publishing house. We had warm conversations on the phone. They brought the situation before the publishing committee and within five days had graciously changed the title of the book. We all parted as friends.

What if I had not done my periodic Internet search until a few weeks or months later? The outcome would probably have been far different. I learned a valuable lesson: increase the routine Internet searches to every two to three months.

You must develop and then protect a brand that sets you apart. Let's take the time to look at how other companies use their branding statements. See how a few words can capture the core essence and philosophy of a company. The fewer the words, the better.

About five minutes ago I pulled the first two advertising fliers I could find in today's newspaper. Two home-improvement giants have brands that communicate volumes. Lowe's® says, "Let's Build Something Together."™ Home Depot® says, "You Can Do It. We Can Help."™ These are well-crafted statements; tag lines that communicate the essence of their business—partnership with the homeowner, coupled with the desire to provide personalized support. Who could ask for more? One statement is only four words and the other is seven words. Now that's what I am talking about.

## Company Name

Ask your lawyer about liability issues before you determine how you are going to create your corporate structure and company name. Do research on the values and limitations, the ups and downs of a sole proprietorship, an LLC, a non-profit, or any other legal structure available to you in your country.

Your company name needs to consist of as few letters and words as possible. When you think of letterheads and business cards, make sure that you select a font that can be easily read in large as well as small fonts. Make sure that the colors you select will look good in black on white. For instance, your company name and logo needs to have visual clarity in a standard facsimile transmission. Pastels may look great in color, but those same colors will be invisible in a fax. Think of all the angles.

If you use the word "the", as in The Freeman Institute®, be careful because it could be listed under either "T" or "F" in the phone book. You can lose customers that way. Some phone companies will list them under both "T" and "F" in the phone book, for a fee. Ask for your phone company's policy on the issue and then make your decision accordingly.

## Company Logo

Spend some time thinking this through. I created a logo once by having five or six inexpensive logo companies on the Internet take a stab at it. I described the thoughts and emotions I wanted people to experience when they saw the logo and I communicated to each designer the general visual concept for the logo. I didn't pay much money for each response and some logo concepts were dreadful. But one artist came through with a winner. He was from Ontario, Canada. He happened to be the cheapest of the bunch. In fact I almost didn't ask him to participate because I thought that he couldn't possibly do anything of substance for me. I was mistaken. I am glad that I gave him the chance to prove himself.

Make sure that the colors used for the logo translate into black and white as well as in full color. Also, remember that if finances are an issue when starting out, one color (black) is the cheapest color to print. A four-color process can get rather costly when considering the charge for printing envelopes, letterheads, business cards, and anything else you may need to have printed. Design a simple logo with simple fonts that work well with a solid blue or black.

---

EXECUTIVE CONCEPTS: Once you have created a company name, a brand, a logo, a business card, and a website, you can start marketing your services. If you are just beginning, do some free-bies for organizations who may already know of you, understanding that they will give you a letter of recommendation and contacts for at least three other people who are their peers, of equal position, in other companies. As your confidence and reputation builds you can develop a fee structure for your services. As personal confidence and customer satisfaction grows, so will your fee.

**BONUS**: You may ask, "What if I have purchased a franchise or am planning to do so? Or what if I have joined or am planning to join a network marketing company?" I am so glad you asked. Franchise companies and network marketing companies have poured enormous resources and time into the development of manuals, systems, and protocol. Follow the bouncing ball. Drawing from vast amounts of experience, they have tried to cover all the bases and anticipate any bumps in the road, handing you a turn-key operation. Plus they have surrounded you with experienced people who can answer your questions and address your concerns. Here's some unsolicited advice: Follow the systems set up in the program you have joined, without any fancy schmancy, extra-curricular stuff from you. Why? Because each system is designed to be successful if duplicated—regardless of your previous experience, skillset, or unique personality style. This is extremely important. The book you now hold in your hands will help you address your attitude and internal level of confidence—within the system or business opportunity you have chosen to work.

**VISION RICH, CASH POOR**: Before purchasing anything substantial—and I mean anything—check online with eBay.com. This will give you a good idea as to the least expensive prices for the equipment you need to purchase, whether it's a telephone, a desk, chair, camera, etc. Be careful. Check the feedback scores of the sellers and the number of transactions they have processed and then bid on whatever you want to purchase. Even if you do not purchase the item on eBay, you will have a benchmark for the best pricing out there.

**BONUS (For Mothers Only):** Most women with children have the "I'm My Kid's Mom" motto as their family brand. Along with that daily reality, there is a new generation of stay-at-home moms taking the entrepreneurial world by storm. T. Foster Jones (magazine writer) states, "These days, when you hear a woman refer fondly to her 'baby,' she just might be talking about her business. No longer content to let motherhood isolate them from or hamper their ability to thrive in the business community, entrepreneurial moms fill an economic niche and have been gaining recognition as a legitimate business force." Including their older child/children in the entrepreneurial pursuit is a part of the business model for many moms.

The nonprofit Center For Women's Business Research (CFWBR), provides us with an ever-expanding picture by communicating, "women are starting new businesses at twice the rate of men and own a 50 percent or greater stake in over 10.6 million U.S. businesses, employing more than 12.8 million people and generating $1.9 trillion in sales. They go on the mention that women of color own 50 percent or more of the 2.4 million firms, employing 1.6 million people and generating $230 billion in sales." (All statistics represent the information available at time of publication. To be sure, the previously mentioned numbers are much higher at the moment you are reading this.)

Here are a few websites, some dispensing current entrepreneurial wisdom and others providing business loans for women . . . especially moms:

- CFWBR.org—Center For Women's Business Research. Invaluable website.

- MIBN.org—Moms In Business Network. An online, women-only networking group.

- AccionUSA.com—A private non-profit organization that offers small business loans of up to $25,000 and financial literacy education to small business owners.

- Count-Me-In.org—provides micro loans from $500 to $10,000 to women who are starting or growing their businesses.

- Mompreneursonline.com—Authors Ellen Parlapiano and Patricia Cole trademarked the term "mompreneurs," giving advice to over 7 million women every month.

- WebMomz.com—Helping thousands of women start their own online business.

- SCORE.org—Counselors to America's small business owners (men and women of all ages included).

## Connecting the Dots:

- USPTO.gov—U.S. Patent and Trademark Office. Once you have come up with a branding statement, do a search on this website to see if it has been taken. If it is available, pay the nominal fee to own it. And then protect it.

- PriceGrabber.com—After checking eBay.com, this is a nice way to compare pricing on anything from office products to apparel.

- CraigsList.org—for both goods and services, bought and sold. Unbelievable resource.

## Entrepreneur Club Option:
## For Personal Reflection and/or Group Discussion

1. Using a thesaurus, pick out action words that describe the vision and mission of your entrepreneurial pursuit.

The words you find will get the creative juices rolling.

2. Develop a series of brief statements that might be the finalists in your quest for a brand. Let yourself go. Look for something that reflects your personality.

3. Nothing is too crazy to put on paper. Bounce the ideas off the creative people who love you and celebrate you.

4. What if you only have 90 seconds to tell someone what you do? Prepare (write) the 90 second script of your business overview and then share it with someone while they time you. Try to get as close to 90 seconds as you possibly can. If you are a part of an Entrepreneur Club, this will be a great exercise for the whole group, with each participant learning how to concisely communicate his or her business passion and also practicing the art of critiquing the other business overviews in an encouraging manner. Memorize your script. Keep memorizing until it can be delivered in a natural, engaging manner. The next time you are on the phone with a prospective client and you have been asked to share what you do . . . you can smile and respond with something like, "Let me give you the 90 second version." And then communicate the script in a timely manner. The person on the other end of the line will be both relieved and impressed.

5. In what ways does your business already stand out like a zebra in the midst of horses? List those unique aspects and then add to that list some creative ideas that can distinguish you even more.

6. In what ways can/will you test the viability of implementing those additional setting-you-apart-from-the-herd ideas?

# CHAPTER SIX

# MARKETING YOURSELF

*If you really want to do something, you'll find a way; if you don't, you'll find an excuse. . . . Dig your well before you are thirsty.*

George C. Fraser

Remember Lauretta? When I was finished talking with her over dinner, I ate another forkful of Chicken Alfredo and then said, "Let's get something straight. No one is more excited about your success than YOU. Not your future agent/manager. Not your future publisher. Not your future publicist. Not your future travel agent. I am very excited about your success, but not even me. You are the one who will have to create the demand for your performances. If nothing is happening, you are the one who is going to have to make it happen."

She nodded in agreement. I'm not sure she totally understood the ramifications of what I meant. But she will.

Marketing is one of the most difficult aspects of creating the demand for your services or goods. It's 10 percent inspiration and 90 percent perspiration.

If we were participating in "Marketing Boot Camp," the sergeant would strut around the room huffing and puffing, "I can't climb into your little tiny heads and hearts to see if you have the work ethic, the credibility, or the follow-up skills to do this thing. But I do know this much. 75 percent of you sniveling wannabees will not make it. Some of you will run out of money. But most of you will be overcome by such negativity that you will quit before six months is up. I can see the lack of conviction in your eyes. You can't handle working from home. Too many distractions."

He stops, puts his hands on his hips, and looks directly at you with a mocking tone, "And I can tell that you are a piece of work. You're probably one of those people who wakes up late, eats breakfast, putters around the house, watches a bit of TV, and then goes to your office to see what needs to be done. By the time you get ready to make the first call, it's already 11:30—oops—potential clients are getting ready for lunch. You can't make any calls until two o'clock because the people you want to reach just might take an early lunch or a late lunch. At two o'clock you might make a few calls. . . ." His voice drops off.

He then steps back surveying the whole group. "Get out of my sight you bunch of babies! Go work for the government or get a job with some other employer!"

## Things Within That May Conspire Against Your Success

This is serious and much of what the sergeant has said is true. Some people spend all their time getting their systems and protocol in place, ready to be successful. Everything is just right. The brand spanking new computer is cutting edge. The filing system is flawless. But they never seem to get around to punching their way out of the four walls that surround them every day. *Ten miles deep, three inches wide.*

A percentage of people are negative nit-pickers. They can brilliantly forecast all the potential potholes ahead. But eventually the "what ifs" get to them. They are so cautious that they never seem to implement the plan.

Other people are hyper-optimistic. They run so fast and in so many directions that they truly don't know where they are going. *Ten miles wide, three inches deep.* They connect with and know hundreds of people. They reach out to people all over the place. But do they ever seem to follow-up and close the deals? Zip. Nada. Zilch.

Any strength overused can and generally will become your greatest vulnerability. Being sensitive is wonderful, but being too sensitive can be a liability. Being blunt is a terrific strength, but being too blunt can turn people off. Fire in a fireplace can set a fabulous mood in the entire room. If you get too close you can get burned. You get the picture.

I am thinking that there must be a happy medium. Kind of like a bulldog with a smile. Everyone leans one way or the other. Be conscious of the direction you lean and then deliberately surround yourself with a couple of other people who lean the other way.

Not too many, but just enough "opposite-leaners" to give you another perspective.

Those who skew to one extreme or the other are likely to fail in their entrepreneurial pursuits, regardless the level of giftedness they possess. They probably need the structure of a corporate environment to properly channel the talents that lie within.

# Ego Issues

When I was working as the mentor/chaplain to the Washington Bullets/Wizards I remember talking with a well-known figure in the NBA. I had casually asked him for his opinion on what it took to make it in the NBA, considering the tens of thousands of young kids who dream and the few who make it.

He turned to me and said, "You have to possess a big ego to play at this level." He paused and then continued, "If a rookie is going to play against Michael Jordan tonight he had better believe that he will beat Michael, or he will end up on a poster in K-Mart with Michael's tongue hanging out doing a slam dunk over the top of him."

A big ego, huh? I am not talking about the "all-elbows" attitude that screams, "Stay out of my way. I'm hot stuff. You're lucky that I permit you to breathe the same air!" Ken Blanchard has stated many times that the word *ego* stands for "Edging God Out." I agree with his assessment.

In the context of the previous statement, however, having a big ego is not being cast in that kind of a negative light. Perhaps we could substitute the word *confidence*.

Assurance in your God-given abilities will give you the energy and creativity to go forward with your dreams. In other words: you have to possess giant confidence in order to play at the level of your dreams. If you choose to accept it, this is one of the occupational hazards of developing your own entrepreneurial pursuit. Why? Because confidence can easily turn into arrogance, especially if you are financially successful.

In the documentary film, *Return To Glory*, world renown neurosurgeon, Dr. Ben Carson gives us a lot to consider, "It all boils down to the way that you see yourself fitting into the big picture.

If you see yourself as a *nothing*, you are not going to have very much self esteem. You are probably not going to move very far in your life. If you see yourself as the *Great One*, you are going to get the big head and you are going to fall. If you see yourself as an *instrument in God's hands*, you recognize that it's about Him and it's not about you. When you recognize that—that is when He can use you. And believe me; He can do a lot more with you than you can do yourself."

Does it mean I am an NBA player trapped in a much smaller 5'10" body? Recently I heard a rather short guy on a comedy show on TV say, "I used to be seven feet tall, but life has beaten me down to five feet!" That's not my particular story, but at this moment I can hear someone in the peanut gallery, with hands cupped about the mouth, yelling, "Yeah, right, Freeman. Don't quit your day job."

The point is, with respect for and acknowledgement of our Creator, we must consistently "play/work" at the professional level of intensity and confidence if we are to become successful, reaching the heights we desire to achieve.

## Marketing 101

Yes, marketing is hard on a number of levels.

1. You are selling yourself and your services. Picture yourself in your jeans or pajamas walking around your home office talking with potential clients all day long on the phone, making sure that you are in tune with the different time zones. If I were a fly on the wall I'd hear you saying something like this, "Mr. Smith, I understand. Thank you for sharing the unique needs of your company with me. I will customize something that will help

you with what you want to accomplish at Acme. You draw the target and I will hit the bulls-eye for you!"

Me, me, me . . . I, I, I . . . I can . . . I will. . . . At the end of the day it can feel like you are just talking about yourself. That can get exhausting and even feel weird. But this is what you have chosen to do. You have to get over it. They are hearing about your goods or services, but they are ultimately "buying" you. Possess the genuine motivation to study your craft or to represent the finest product line so that you can help others win. Provide excellent customer service in addition to that and you will succeed beyond your wildest expectations. Someone once told me, "There's a fine line between arrogance and confidence and you have to walk it." I'm not sure that I have always walked that line very well, but those are words worth considering.

2. It is nice to find someone else to "sell" you and your services, but that isn't always a realistic option while starting up a business venture, unless you have tons of money. Very few seasoned agents or marketers will work on a commission basis. In terms of agents there are some wonderful and pleasant exceptions out there, but you will discover that many agents and publicists are lazy. There, I've said it. If you are good at what you do, agents will stroke your ego with grandiose promises, trying to lock you into an exclusive contract. Most agents lack long-term creativity and passion. That may sound harsh, but I suggest that you check it out for yourself. (Later I will share an agent idea that may work very well for you.) At a certain level it might be important for you to develop an exclusive relationship with someone who has proven to be a hard and smart worker on your behalf.

That person is a rare jewel and deserves to be compensated well for his or her efforts.

3. Markets will change. What was in demand last year may not even be a blip on this year's radar screen. You will have to work very hard at personal development so that you will not get comfortable with what you are good at this year. You must keep reading and studying. Keep up with current events and technology. Become multiculturally astute. Take the time to learn about other cultures. In the fourth century, Augustine said, "Seek to understand before seeking to be understood." When you travel internationally, spend extra days before or after the event; dressing down and getting out of your four-star hotel, mixing with the culture. Regardless of your chosen field of interest, read books and periodicals about other communities you will serve. Not all readers are leaders. But all leaders are readers. Are you a leader in your industry? Do you really want to be a leader in your industry? If so, read.

4. Sometimes the telephone weighs five hundred pounds. Some days will feel flat. It will feel like every telephone call you make is truly long distance. Other days will be full of excitement and positive responses. You must learn to treat both success and failure as imposters. Maintain an even keel. Keep a sense of humor about yourself. Regardless of how you feel, get moving in a positive direction and you'll start feeling the juice. Success breeds more success.

5. Keep the pipeline full. Having jobs scheduled six months ahead is beguiling. It's tempting to take your hand off the throttle. You must make sure that there are opportu-

nities opening up nine to twelve, even fifteen, months ahead. Some organizations make decisions a year in advance. You need to identify the key decision-makers and the way they make decisions. Celebrate with some time off when you have achieved a particular goal. If you are in the early stages of the start-up, you may not have the luxury of taking too many days off at any given time until things are a wee bit more established. Cost-effective mini-vacations are the way to go. Be creative with your celebrations. An afternoon at the park, a movie or a museum visit with your spouse, during your normally prime business hours, send a very powerful signal of gratitude and appreciation for his or her emotional support.

6. Become the best in a particular industry. Learn the culture of that industry by interviewing some of the people who work in it. Among other topics of interest, ask them, "What gives you the most pain in your job?" Once you have identified the common issues, develop a customized approach that will speak their language and will hit a bulls-eye for your customers every time. Your work will be in such demand that you may never have to move out of that industry.

Every industry has an association. (You've heard of AOWHERI, haven't you? It's the Association of One-armed Wallpaper Hangers who Experience Random Itching.) Most associations have an annual convention, or at least regional get-togethers. It would a valuable expenditure of your time to be a keynote speaker or the facilitator of a breakout workshop session or two. You may be able to barter for a booth, as partial payment for your services. The sales from the booth and potential business from some of the participants who love your work should help to offset your time and expenses.

7. Colleges and universities host student events and faculty/staff development programs throughout the year. Develop a seminar or presentation that reaches your target audience and then communicate the essence of that program to the appropriate coordinators at the educational institution.

8. Someone once said, "If you fail at marketing yourself you are either too lazy or too proud." There may be some other nuances to that statement, but those are words worth embroidering. Laziness is easy to measure and attack. Pride is a much more difficult thing to identify, measure, or attack. Pride in one's work is admirable, but the pride that keeps one from stepping out of his or her personal comfort zone needs to be confronted. An entrepreneurial pursuit will be a laboratory, perfectly designed to smoke out this type of unhealthy pride.

9. David Asche, a friend of mine, was driving to work one day in Southern California. He did a double-take when he saw a guy in a sharp looking suit standing next to his shiny BMW beside the busy highway, holding up a sign: WILL WORK FOR SIX FIGURES. There were a few cars on the side of the road getting the man's resumé. Intrigued, David pulled over and asked him how it was going. He stated that he already had several appointments booked for job interviews and was confident he would have no trouble landing a job. That's a healthy, "out-of-the-box" expression of the entrepreneurial spirit! Creativity. Perseverance. Willing to take a risk. Willing to place himself outside of his comfort zone; even look

like a fool. Crazy like a fox. That kind of ingenuity can capture a job. But I also have the sense that he could deliver the goods once hired. By the way, the guy was looking for a marketing position. If nobody loves you, create the demand!

10. Never underestimate the power of word-of-mouth advertising. There's a lot of history about companies that do not advertise in the traditional way. For instance, up until January 2006, I understand that Krispy Kreme (donuts) relied primarily upon word-of-mouth advertising—never using TV commercials, billboards, radio ads, or print ads. With increased competition that marketing strategy has since changed, but there is a lesson to be learned: focus first on the quality of your product or service. If it's excellent, your satisfied customers will spread the word.

11. A statement that resounds in my head daily: *"Freeman, you are either hiring yourself or firing yourself every day."*

12. I have taped another statement to the top of my computer: "Do first what you dread the most." Need I say more?

## Fax and Email

Yes, I do need to say more. We are living in a wonderful era of human history. There's an upside and a downside to most things. But all in all, this is a wonderful time to be alive. The good old days included no air conditioning, horse and buggy, and the only running water was when you ran and got it with a pail. I'm not interested in going back to the good old days unless I plan for it, camping with an air mattress and a tent.

We are living in an era of microwave ovens, high definition televisions, and cells phones. It's easy to get spoiled by all of the conveniences at our disposal. We complain when we have to add another thirty seconds to the re-heating of yesterday's leftovers or when our cell phone drops its signal in the middle of a conversation.

Some days I sit at my desk while talking with a potential client. I have sent the requested email, and while waiting, we both comment about how long it is taking for the email to go through— we have been waiting for twenty to thirty seconds.

"Got it yet?"

"Let me try again . . . nope." Silence.

"Sheesh, I wonder what's the matter. Let me make sure that I've got the correct email address. What was it again?"

"Here it is. It just came through."

You're grinning. You know exactly what I am talking about. Impatience is the official emotion of this era.

Email is a powerful tool. In the previous scenario, I am talking with a potential client and within a relatively short period of time the interested person has received what I affectionately call my *Digital Propaganda Letter*, complete with hyperlinks. She can review my video clips, seminar program overviews, endorsements, my bio, and anything else that is needed before an intelligent decision can be made. I have verified that the email has been received. It sure beats mailing a package and waiting several days to make sure the postal service has done its job.

I started The Freeman Institute® in 1994, before the Internet was as pervasive as it is today. My main tools were the fax machine, the phone, and the US Mail. I didn't have enough money to print and mail brochures when I first started, so I decided that the telephone and a one-page fax would be my primary marketing tools.

Why a one page fax? Have you ever had an unsolicited eleven-pager come through? It can make you grumpy. A one-page facsimile can communicate everything you need to get to the next level of discussion with the intended recipient. No need for a cover sheet.

A fax transmission doesn't depend upon expensive glossy paper with four-color printing. Faxing depends entirely upon strong, simple graphics and text that is easy to read. Plus, some people are so numb to emails (because of all the spam) that a one-page fax has re-emerged as a novel means of communication.

At first I had two telephone lines. On one line I called people to tell them about my services and then asked them for their fax number. I had a Panasonic fax machine, a workhorse that took 57–60 seconds to transmit a complete page. As the page was going through to the previous caller, I would start the ritual all over again with another potential client. It was boring and methodical. And I didn't even have a website.

Business began to trickle in. People started calling, "Hello. I received a fax about your seminar services. I was wondering if you could tell me a little more about your Conflict Resolution Seminar. There are a few people around here that don't get along with each other very well. . . ."

Many evenings I would go to the local library and search through the books with business listings in the DC/Baltimore region. Since they were reference books, I wasn't allowed to take check them out. I couldn't afford the cost of feeding the copy machine at the library, so I hand wrote fax numbers on blank sheets of paper, three columns wide. I copied hundreds, no thousands, of fax numbers during those first few years. Then

I would go back to my home. Because I could never quite figure out the fax-broadcasting feature on the machine, I would send faxes—one at a time—while watching TV. Every 57 seconds another fax would go through, addressed to the company training director. I was multi-tasking before the word was invented.

The next day I would call each company to make sure that the training director had received the fax. Slowly, but surely, work began to dribble in. No one told me to do it this way, but it was the only way I could reach out to the most companies in the least amount of time, on a limited budget.

We now have email as the primary communication tool. Faxing may still work for you, as long as you are calling people before or after faxing a one-page overview of your services. If you broadcast faxes you will create enemies of the very people you want to serve.

Emails can contain hyperlinks that guide a willing recipient to specific pages on your website. You can call someone on the phone. Tell them what you can offer their organization and then ask for permission to send an email. "Permission Marketing" is far more successful than spamming three hundred thousand people at one time. In fact, spamming will destroy your credibility and your business faster than most anything else you can do to facilitate an "anti-success" business development strategy.

My *Digital Propaganda Letter* has done wonders for my business. It has proven to be one of the most powerful marketing tools I use. If you would like a copy, email me with your request (contact information on page 201) and I will gladly send it to you. I delete spam with a vengeance, so make sure that your request is clearly stated in the subject line. "I read your book and I want your TFI digital propaganda letter."

Whenever I email a willing recipient, I always place the person's name and organization in the main body of the email, along with a prepared personal note placed just prior to the generic letter. I have it down to a science. I can customize and send an email within twenty to thirty seconds. You can break my record once you develop your own style of copying and pasting.

An email is much faster, easier to customize, and contains more information than a one-page fax. The Internet has dramatically changed the way my business is marketed.

One cautionary note regarding the Internet: once your website is up and running, you will receive many calls and emails offering you opportunities to invest your hard-earned money in Internet advertising. I am sure that I have turned down some wonderful plans that work. But after most of what I hear or read, my immediate thought is, *On one hand, I can utilize this costly Internet banner ad marketing idea, or on the other hand, I can flush a ton of money down the toilet. Hmmm, which one should I choose?*

## Hire a Pre-Teenager

Abigail Van Buren ("Dear Abby" author) once stated, "If you want your children to keep their feet on the ground, put some responsibility on their shoulders." Here's a smart idea that includes the fax machine, your one-page "propaganda letter," and a family member or a neighbor kid. Identify one of your children (assuming you have children), a nephew or niece, or the next-door neighbor's kid who might be interested in a business proposal. Agree to pay the kid five dollars an hour, plus you will give him or her a 5 to 10 percent finder's fee for any business that comes in through the fax marketing program. Monitor the calls you receive. "How did you hear about us? You received a fax? Great!"

Set aside a thousand dollars. Ask the youngster to fax for an hour a day for just five days a week. That means you'll be paying twenty-five dollars a week for forty weeks, plus any finder's fee. Do you realize that an overall investment of a thousand dollars gives you approximately ten months of marketing? Get two fax machines working at the same time, and the youngster can get twice as much done in one hour.

Just for fun, let's do the math. Let's say that with two fax machines, a youngster can conservatively send eighty faxes in an hour. Based upon an hour a day for five days, four hundred faxes can be sent in a week. If my math is correct, after forty weeks about sixteen thousand faxes have been sent! That's a lot of follow-up calls. A mere 1 percent return on investment is 160 potential clients—sixteen a month . . . enough to make anyone happy. Your results may be different, but it's worth considering.

Think about it. You are providing a job for a pre-teenager who isn't old enough yet to be paid the minimum wage for asking the all-important question, "Do you want fries with that?" It would be a bonus if you could get one of your own children to do this. You would minimize the money you'd be shelling out anyway for candy, video games, and other "essentials," and your child would feel a greater part of the family enterprise.

If you are reading this book as a teenager, or as someone with no pre-teenagers, you'll figure out some other cost-effective way of doing this.

I am against mass fax broadcasting because I think it turns off most potential clients. But try sending one fax at a time with a hand-written note at the top (To: The Training Director or the title of the person you want to reach) or you can use sticky notes on the upper left-hand corner of the page, and each fax sent can even be personalized. It may take a few moments longer, but it can revolutionize the way people respond to your efforts. This can be especially powerful if you or your spouse (assuming you are married) calls the next day to make sure that the fax was received by the right person and expresses the desire to answer any questions. There's no substitute for the personal touch.

I have utilized this idea, and it has worked very well. Even if only one event comes through in ten months, it's a winner. When I write one of those 5 percent checks the huge smile on my face pales, compared to the one thousand watt glow emanating from the young recipient's joyful face.

## Telephone Basics

When following up with someone who has expressed interest in what you do, never leave the burden for returning the call on the other person. It sets up an awkward situation. What if the person gets busy and forgets? Make it your own responsibility, even if the other person says that he or she will get back to you.

Say something like this, "Both of us have crazy schedules. It is real easy for me to get back to you. When is the best time? Next month?" A month gives the clear signal that there is no pressure coming from you. In some cases, I'll even go out as far as suggesting two to three months for the call-back. The other person generally becomes more proactive, responding with, "Oh, no, not that long. We can talk again much earlier than that. How about next Thursday?" I then ask for the best time of day and write it down. When the other person realizes that I am writing it down, he or she knows that there is going to be a return call on a specific date at a specific time.

I have a cheap alarm clock near my desk. If I have promised to do a follow-up call on a Thursday afternoon at two o'clock, I will set the alarm clock first thing in the morning. Sometimes I am so preoccupied with another project that when the alarm goes off, I have to take a look at my appointment book to determine what it was reminding me to do.

When I call back at the appointed day and time, I generally say something like, "Hello Tina. This is Joel Freeman. You may remember two weeks ago we talked about _____. At that time, you mentioned that we should talk today. I hope your day is going well for you. Is this a good moment for you?"

When you have called someone and get voice mail, leave your message once—and that's it. At the end of your message say something like, "You can try to reach me and I can try to reach out to you. Perhaps we'll connect in the middle." It may sound simple and even a wee bit corny, but that statement gives you permission to keep calling back until you make a live connection with that particular individual. Never leave the ultimate responsibility with them to get back to you. It may never happen. Or if they do call back, you may not even remember who they are and why you called them in the first place. This can be both embarrassing and unprofessional.

If you have called back a few times and feel like you just might be bugging the person, say something like this and really mean it, "There is a fine line between keeping in touch and being a pest. I never want to cross that line with you." The other person generally responds with, "Hey, no problem at all. My schedule has been crazy. I am glad that you are keeping in touch. . . ." Being a pest will repel, but keeping a zero-pressure connection may ultimately bring about a win/win scenario.

William Wadsworth Longfellow once stated, "Perseverance is a great element of success. If you knock *long* enough and *loud* enough at the gate, you are sure to wake up somebody."

*Long* and *loud* may cause one to creep toward the "pest syndrome," but I do think Longfellow makes a valid point. Perseverance may or may not pay off, but it sure increases the odds of a successful outcome. It's up to you to discover the balance. And you will.

---

**EXECUTIVE CONCEPTS:** Within the context of time management, multiplication is better than addition. Look for ways to multiply your efforts. There are only so many "awake hours" in one day. You and I can physically be in only one place at one time. Look for pursuits that help you to be in many places at one time. That's why I write books, along with producing CDs and DVDs. I can focus on the writing process for weeks or months knowing that when the manuscript is finished, I never have to touch it again. It then goes out and does what it does. Over time, with ten to twelve items completed and out there, I am building a residual income that is almost like an annuity. At this moment I am in my home in Maryland, while my books are currently in twenty-eight different translations/editions around the world. I knew this is what I wanted to happen, but I never anticipated that it would be this many. My new goal is fifty different translations/foreign editions.

I currently have three online training courses that I have co-created with HR Train, a progressive company in Jericho, NY. The beauty of an online course is that a company of any size, with branches in regions around the world can use it. This means that twenty thousand employees of a large company can be utilizing one of my online courses (diversity, conflict resolution, and violence prevention) while my wife and I are on a cruise. The international "hybrid" marketing strategy is already developed for *Diversity: The Value of Mutual Respect.* The online diversity course, coupled with the book version (working on it) and live seminar presentation is destined to be an international powerhouse—for more information: www.greatEseminars.com.

Be attracted to things that are central to your passions and still bring income to your family—without the need for your presence. If you can make money only when you show up, you are limiting your earning power and you are also limiting your personal global impact.

I do not know how the multiplication idea fits into your specific field of interest, but perhaps you do. And if you don't know, keep wrestling with it until you figure it out.

For instance, if you are an artist (painter), consider making high-end prints and framed, limited edition (numbered) giclée reproductions of a few of your finest works. Develop a DVD demonstrating your painting technique.

Create postcards and/or all-occasion cards of your finest images. Do a search on the Internet for the least expensive printing companies that specialize in high quality postcards. Ask them to send samples of their work. On the back of each postcard print your website and a brief overview of the inspiration you felt when painting the image. Every time a postcard is sent out, someone else is paying the postage to help you market your paintings. In other words, every postcard mailed by someone else is being mailed to a new potential customer for you.

Get the picture? They paid you for the postcards and now they are paying to mail them to their friends and relatives. Projects like these fit into your passion as a painter, but also can provide a small income stream without the need for you to be present when the cash register rings in your online store.

**VISION RICH, CASH POOR:** Never buy a fax machine or printer until you have determined how much the ink cartridges will cost. (Think about the razor/razor blades concept.) Research the cost of ink for specific hardware on the Internet first, and then read the research on the machines with the least expensive cartridges. In our offices we own a few Epson C62 printers, which do a great job. They are not the latest and greatest, but they do a fine enough job for our purposes. I don't know if they are even available anymore. We recently received twelve black ink cartridges and six color ink cartridges in one order (total of eighteen cartridges) for less than fifty bucks, shipping included. Incredible! Go to your local office supply store and compare what you would get for the same amount of money.

**BONUS:** If you have a small targeted mailing for prospective customers, consider purchasing many sheets of one penny stamps. Place the proper number of stamps on each envelope. It will be extra work, but it doesn't cost any more than normal to do the mailing. Every envelope will stand out, causing your customers to be intrigued. Hopefully they will be curious enough to take a look at your information and hire you or purchase your product(s).

## Connecting the Dots:

The following are examples of some value-added items that we created or have brought under The Freeman Institute® umbrella. I select items that do not take my attention away from my main purpose, but that still create an opportunity for average people to enhance their lives with unique quality products. I will list some of the websites below. They are self-explanatory. An updated and complete list of hyperlinked websites can be found at: www.TheFreemanEnterprises.com.

- FreemanStuff.com—All of the resources (books, DVDs, CDs) produced by The Freeman Institute®.

- BlackHistoryPostCards.com—Postcards I have developed from The Freeman Institute® Black History Collection.

- AstoundingImage.com—Larger-than-normal "Earth At Night" all-occasion cards I have developed, along with stunning museum-quality wall art.

- DiversitySeminars.com—The online courses I have co-developed with HR Train, addressing: diversity, workplace violence, and conflict resolution.

- FastMortgageReduction.com—A remarkable, not-your-typical way to pay off a 30-year mortgage in 8 to 12 years, without refinancing and with no impact on the monthly budget. Yes, I was also intrigued when I first saw this. It's different and it works.

- SmokeEscapeHood.com—The inexpensive, easy-to-use Smoke Escape Hood that should be a requirement for every home and office building, especially second floor and above. It's the one product I hope you never use.

- JohariGame.com—The game that corporations around the world use to enhance teamwork, leadership, diversity, and intra-organizational issues.

- SaveEnergy101.com—The technology that will permit you to save up to 25 percent on your monthly electric bill for homes (single-phase) and larger office buildings (three-phase).

- ItTakesABusiness.com, ItTakesASchool.com, ItTakesACountry.com, or ItTakesACity.org—An all-day regional or national (small developing nation) leadership/personal and staff development seminar event for various venues.

## Entrepreneur Club Option:
## For Personal Reflection and/or Group Discussion

1. Make a list of all the spin-off products that you can produce.

2. Develop a timeline and then start creating these projects, one by one until you have exhausted every possible means of leveraging what you have.

3. What kind of time will you commit every day to your vision?

4. How will you reward yourself when you reach certain predetermined goals? Fill in the blanks: "When I reach
   _____, I will _____."
   If you have a family, involve them in the celebration and reward.

5. How does the use of the fax and email fit into your marketing plans?

6. Check out the e-zine concept. Think about having a spot on your website for people to give you their email addresses so that you can send them a periodic email loaded with helpful information. Once permission is given, you can periodically stay on the radar screens of thousands of people who may eventually open other doors of opportunity for you. Make sure that 97.5 percent of what you communicate is practical, usable advice. Don't make it one big advertisement for your business. People will unsubscribe and your reputation will be toast.

# CHAPTER SEVEN

# ENHANCING YOUR INFLUENCE

*A great pleasure in life is doing what other
people say you cannot do.*

Walter Gagehot

What is your entrepreneurial pursuit? Fixing computers? Professional speaking? Lawn and garden? Decorating? Art? Music? Writing? Marketing? Remodeling? Consulting? Singing? Plumbing? Dentistry? Whatever it is, why not be a recognized expert in your field?

One of the best ways to establish yourself is to write a booklet or even a book about your arena of expertise. Thomas Edison once said, "If we did all the things we are capable of, we would literally astound ourselves." Even though you may feel inadequate as a writer, you will be surprised by the ways you will be stretched—both personally and professionally. Put up your antennas, and you will see how many writers' club are in your community. Writers' clubs can provide a great source of encouragement and practical guidance.

Remember Lauretta? I suggested that she embark upon even greater research regarding the history of negro spirituals. I loaned her a few vintage nineteenth-century items from The Freeman Institute® Black History Collection. These genuine items contain pre-copyrighted images and content that she can use for her booklet. Images and vintage content like this will give her booklet a greater aura of authenticity, if and when she is ready to write it.

Let's take a closer look at your booklet. Check out eBay, or some other auction service, as a great place to start when trying to pick up a few rare items that can provide a historic backdrop to your thesis. Make the booklet experiential. Tell your story.

What drew you to your specific field of interest? Who mentored you? Who are the pioneers/inventors, and what were their struggles? What makes you unique in this particular field of interest? What have been some of your greatest personal challenges? The answers to these questions will get you started.

Surprise people with excellent, engaging content. Write a few chapters and then walk away from the manuscript for a while. When you come back in a few days or weeks later to read what you have written, you will know immediately whether or not it feels right.

I have written chapters in the middle of the night. Everything flowed so well. I had such a wonderful writing experience that I would go to sleep developing my Pulitzer Prize acceptance speech. At 10:15 the next morning, the same stuff was awful—dreadful! *What was I thinking?* Well, the Pulitzer Prize is still safe!

Don't give up before you start. Know that if this is your first writing experience you will probably have to do four or five rewrites before it has the crispness and readability that you desire. Budget this reality in the account of your mind and enjoy the process. My first book took five rewrites. By the third rewrite I was ready to throw it in the trashcan. I have gotten better over the years, but when I started out, the learning curve was straight up.

The contents of the book you now hold in your hands have been gurgling around in me for years. I wrote 90 percent of this book in four days. This was an unusual experience for me. I was in such a creative zone that sentences and paragraphs poured out of me onto my laptop screen. During the writing process, thoughts and ideas were bombarding me from all sides. At times I had to literally stop typing and write key words on a piece of paper to make sure that those thoughts would be included in the manuscript at a later time. This has never happened before and may never happen again quite like that.

A good way to test the metal of your almost-finished manuscript is to find a quiet spot in your home and read it out loud. You will discover much about the reader-friendliness of your work. If it doesn't sound just right keep changing the sentence structure until it rolls off your tongue smoothly. Trust your gut and your red pen as you make the necessary changes. Readability is extremely important if you want to connect with your audience. This will also help to prepare you for the audio version of your book, designed to reach busy professionals, people who can't read, and the sight-impaired.

Everyone has his or her own style. Borrow stylistic ideas from others, but don't be a copycat. Be comfortable with your unique approach to writing.

If others have written books on a similar topic, you must answer the question, "How is my book different from all others dealing with the same subject matter?"

For instance, a lot of people have written about becoming or being an entrepreneur. Before writing this book I had to ask some tough questions, like "What will make this particular book different?" I have a three-point response to that question, but perhaps you can help. What has engaged you to stay with my book up to this point?

Let's discuss another topic. Hard cover or soft cover? It depends. The perceived value for hard cover is greater. Even though it is more expensive to manufacture, you can charge more per copy. If your primary purpose is retail sales or greater credibility, that's the way to go.

If your main purpose is bulk sales or giving away free review copies, soft cover may be the best way to go. Weigh the options and make a decision. If you want a soft cover version, get it perfect-bound (regular paperback binding)—never saddle-stitched (stapled) unless it is a small informational booklet or an insert with a CD or DVD.

Establish your purpose for writing. *Why am I doing this?* If it is merely to make money, you may be barking up the wrong tree. The odds are against it. Truth be told, you might as well spend the same hours flipping hamburgers at the fast food joint down the street. Chances are you'll make more money. You will probably not break even financially on the first print run. Last I heard, only 5 percent of all books published go beyond five thousand copies sold. The mortality rate of published books is high.

But it will be worth it, because having a book or booklet published will open doors for you like very few other things you can do to enhance your influence. What if a copy of your book helps to open the door for you to get a job that brings in a total of twenty-five thousand dollars to your bank account? It's a hypothetical question that you will never know the answer to until you try it. And that could be only the beginning.

You will give away many books initially. Take that into account. You have to seed the field before you get a crop. You know the recipe for stupidity or insanity: *planting just a few seeds and expecting a bumper crop.* Your chances increase with the number of seeds planted. This is a great way to establish and broaden your credibility. Just make sure that you plant the seeds in the right soil.

If you are, let's say, a dentist, a chiropractor, or a plumber, a free autographed copy of your book for every new customer is something that sets you apart from your competition. How many others in your line of work can compete with that unique offer?

Once the book is completed, give away a chapter or two on your website. Leave the web surfer wanting more. (Check out the way I do it on CreateTheDemand.com.) If the content in the first couple of chapters is compelling, it will significantly increase your online sales.

## Contacting the Key Decision-Maker

Let's get back to the topic at hand. Call before sending the book to a key decision-maker (talk show host, seminar coordinator, etc.) so that you establish voice contact with the individual you want to receive the book. This pre-qualifying telephone call permits you to make sure that you are sending the book to the right person, and it also gives you an opportunity to make sure that it will be valued by the recipient.

The follow-up telephone call is also very important. Contact the same individual four to six days after the book has been sent. "Hello Terry, I'm calling to see if the Postal Service did their job. I know that you haven't had the time to review it yet, but I just wanted to make sure that the book I sent you arrived in one piece." This is a warm, non-threatening way to make sure that your book is in the right hands.

Terry responds, "Yes, I am quite sure that it arrived. Hold on a moment, let me look. . . . Yes, here it is!" You now have accomplished something that sets you apart from all other authors. Your book is the hands of a key decision-maker—and you are on the phone at the same time. A rare and powerful combination.

If you are on the speaking, performing, or singing circuit (some do all three), with your book you now have an "upsell" item in the back of the room. If, let's say, two hundred people each pay fifteen dollars for your book, you have made an extra three thousand bucks. And you may have even paid for a major portion of your printing costs! Plus you are confident that those two hundred people will show the autographed book to two or three others, some of whom may make an online purchase of the same book while visiting your website.

What is the compelling reason for people to purchase from you? On your website you state, "Where else can you get this book autographed by the author?" Internet surfers are generally savvy buyers. They know how to get books at the cheapest possible place on the Internet. Your offer to personalize the book will set you apart from anyone else offering the book at a cheaper price, including Amazon, Borders, Barnes & Noble, and other well-known online stores. The point being that you increase your profits when you sell it yourself.

If you and I were discussing the topic of writing and publishing in the mid 1990s, I would have counseled you to get your booklet published by a recognized book publisher. I am thankful to have this book published by Authentic Publishing.

In many cases it is an excellent idea. Why? Publishers are a great option because they bring on an editor to enhance the reader-friendliness of your manuscript. They also take on the financing of the cover graphics, page layout and design. They take the risk, spending money on marketing and generally have a much wider access to distribution . . . with more established inroads to book-stores and department stores around the country and the world. These are all very important aspects to consider.

Technology has changed all the rules. The advent of the Internet has permitted us "little people" to have a vehicle for marketing and distributing our own books without having a huge percentage carved out by a middle person.

In the Bonus Material, *If I Can Write, You Can Write*, I share some advice and some websites regarding the writing, graphic design, fabrication, and marketing of your first booklet or book.

One of the most important things to remember: **Events sell books**. If you have a booth at a convention, make sure that you have some unique "schtick" to set your booth apart. Speaking at breakout sessions will drive conference participants to your booth, and they will tell others. By the third day of the conference, people will be coming to the convention hall making a beeline to your booth.

Here's another thought—what if you crafted and wordsmithed the contents and design of the booklet for bulk purchases? Single sales are wonderful, but bulk sales are fantastic! Some corporations like to "private label" inexpensive booklets.

Let's say Acme Corporation likes what you have done, and they want to get a copy in the hands of their employees, all eighteen thousand of them! Here is where private labeling can pay off for you. You will want to make sure that there is a page or two near the front available for an open letter from the president of Acme. You will also want to design the cover so that the Acme company logo can be placed in one of the corners. Do a special print run. Even if you clear only 75 cents on each copy, it's enough to make your day. Am I right? Caution: do not get greedy. You'll lose the sale. I'd rather have a small percentage of something than 100 percent of nothing, wouldn't you?

Why self-publish your book? The value of self-publishing is that you can do what you want when you want to do it. You are not restricted by a publisher. Most of the larger publishing houses will be far more restrictive regarding the "private-labeling" of your book. Plus they will generally want to retain the lion's share of the finances.

The value of being published through one of the larger publishing houses is that they will provide you with an editor who can increase the life-changing quality of your manuscript. Plus they can get your book in the mainstream bricks-n-mortar bookstores. Ultimately it's your call.

Once your book or booklet is printed, you can add another item to your resumé/obituary-type stuff: *author*. The booklet now becomes an expensive business card, setting you apart from all others. Like many farmers, you'll be "out-standing" in your field.

---

**EXECUTIVE CONCEPTS:** Writing will clarify your thinking and speaking like nothing else you have ever done. You will be forced to research and verify things you have taken for granted. You will be stretched both personally and professionally. Even if you never sell a book, you must do this for your own internal benefit. This is your primary purpose. Whatever you write becomes part of the legacy you leave to the next generation.

**BONUS (For Inventors Only):** In the early 1980s, the immensely popular Atari 2600 video game system boasted game cartridges such as Space Invaders, Breakout, Adventure, Outlaw, and Space Wars. I know that I am dating myself, but I remember spending hours playing these games. After a few months of using the standard hand-held joystick control, the wrist on my left arm began to experience some sharp pain from absorbing the shock of my up and down, back and forth movements. It was a brutally unforgiving controller.

On the morning of June 16, 1982, an invention idea popped into my head. I drew it on a piece of paper and hand wrote as complete an overview of my idea as possible. I called it the "Wrist Fatigue Eliminator for Atari Joystick Controls."

How did it work? It was a 15" x 15" x ½" piece of Plexiglas (the prototype was made of wood), with a hole in the middle for the joystick controller to be set and thin strips of Velcro to hold the controller securely in place. It was held close to the abdomen and could be used right or left handed because of a specially positioned hole above the joystick designed to absorb the stress and shock of moving the joystick. Everyone who saw it thought it would be a hit.

After a lot of research I finally submitted the idea to the US Patent and Trademark Office (serial #389294) on July 29, 1983. It was the first time I did something like this, and I didn't use a lawyer. I do not have a glamorous ending to this story because the technology of joystick controls advanced during the time it took for me to move through the various stages of the patent process. My Wrist Fatigue Eliminator was no longer a viable product for the marketplace, and I had to abandon the idea. However, I still have the paperwork, graphic designs, photographs, and prototypes in my office. Here are some wisdom lessons I learned from my experiences. You can view them as mere suggestions:

1. Don't tell anyone about your idea until you have enclosed it in an envelope and sent it back to yourself via Registered Mail. An unopened envelope with the date hand stamped all over the sealed flap of the envelope is a way of establishing the original date of conception.

2. I am not a big fan of the companies with TV ads asking inventors to submit their ideas. Verify the history and integrity of any such company before unveiling your invention. You might be better finding a trusted friend or two who can give you the objectivity needed to see if it is a viable idea that can be successful in the marketplace.

3. Getting an idea from your brain to the marketplace is an extremely difficult endeavor. Here are some suggestions on things you can do while going through the long patent process: Research the manufacturing costs, develop the business plan, look for investors, and ascertain the most creative and workable marketing concepts. Each point in the entire chain needs to work. For instance, the manufacturing cost has to permit enough of a markup so that the distributors can make enough money to make it worth their while. The quantity of items manufactured at one time will determine the per-item cost. Also, most retail stores need at least a 100 percent markup (some are demanding more), along with a product size that doesn't take up too much space on their shelves. Researching all of the above-mentioned aspects will provide the kind of reality check that will help you determine the viability of such a product. The Internet is changing all the rules, so

research the "manufacturing-and-taking-the-product-to-market-yourself" option.

4. Caution: If your product is successful, some large corporation or a company from another country may steal it, tying you up in litigation for years. If your product is unsuccessful, you will invest a lot of time and money, with no marketable product as a result. Possible solution: You may be better served cutting a deal with a reputable company that can give you a per-sale royalty for the manufacture and distribution of your product.

5. No reputable retail outlet will even listen to you about distributing your invention until you can prove that you own the patent, so procuring the patent is an important early step.

6. Have fun with the process and follow it through until you have satisfactorily explored every avenue. Persevere, with wisdom. I wish you all the best.

## Connecting the Dots:

- PrintingForGood.com—Great place to self-publish your book. As an individual you can go to a printer and get a price. This company, however, can go to the same printer and get a much cheaper price. Why? Because they get millions of books printed for people. This is one of the few times that the middle person gets a cheaper price, allowing the author to win.

- Black101.com—The Freeman Institute® Black History Collection designed to educate and inspire young people. I loaned a few pieces to Lauretta.

## Entrepreneur Club Option:
## For Personal Reflection and/or Group Discussion

1. What makes your book different from all others on the selected topic?

2. What are some of the ways you can leverage and utilize the booklet you will write?

3. How can you help promote it? Are you willing to go on the "rubber chicken" circuit? (Most events you will speak at will serve chicken.)

4. Why would anyone want to read a book written by you? In other words, what gives you the credibility to write about a chosen subject?

# REINVENTING YOURSELF

*Champions aren't made in the gyms. Champions are made*
*from something they have deep inside of them—a desire,*
*a dream, a vision. They have last-minute stamina, they have*
*to be a little faster, they have to have the skill, and the will.*
*But the will must be stronger than the skill.*

Muhammad Ali

A common question posed to young people is, "What are you going to do when you grow up?" Decades ago that was a valid question. Today's marketplace technology is changing all the rules. Other factors conspire; and before we know it, a giant segment of industry is carved out, never to be replaced.

The question, "What are you going to do when you grow up?" has become more complicated. The average teenager today may have to change careers up to four times before he or she retires. That's one of the reasons why it is important to embrace the personal and business reinvention concept.

Remember those long-playing (LP) albums? The record industry had billions of dollars invested in the manufacturing, packaging, and marketing of 45s and LPs. Except for an occasional yard sale, they are currently hard to find. Why? Because a little thing called digital technology came along and changed everything. The folks invested in the 12-inch records had to reinvent themselves—almost overnight—with the introduction of the CD and digital technology. If you were born before 1960, you probably got a bit cranky the first time you had to purchase a CD player. But now you wouldn't dream of going back to the old technology. Your perspective about the way music is delivered has been reinvented.

## A Personal Story

How have I been challenged in this area? Glad you asked. There have been times when the seminar side of things has virtually dried up for me. I have facilitated many seminars for government agencies in the Washington, DC region. The fiscal year of the American government runs from the beginning of October to the end of September. In recent years there has been what they call a "Continuing Resolution" (CR). This is government-speak. Our public servants on Capitol Hill can't get their act together to fund the new budget for the government. So instead of shutting the government down, they allow the government to function until the new budget is approved, but nothing new is funded for months. A real morale booster! Seminar training is the last thing on their minds.

Sometimes I will have seminar events in the pipeline for nine months ahead. I know that the family bills are taken care of for that period of time. All of a sudden the phone will ring and an apologetic voice on the other end states, "Dr. Freeman, we're sorry, but our plans have changed. We have cancelled the convention for November. We'll keep you in our plans for next year's convention."

And then, as if a conspiracy has been triggered, the phone will ring more times that same week with similar messages for three or four other high-paying events. All of a sudden, the smug smile is wiped off my face, and I have to start thinking what can be done to refill the pipeline and create more business.

It's during these times that new ideas emerge. Mind you, when things are rolling along, I am quite comfortable. Is that true for you? I tend to take my hand off The Freeman Institute® throttle. My creativity tends to flow into my non-profit adventures. It isn't until I am in tough times that my creative juices start flowing back toward The Freeman Institute®. I guess there is a side benefit to dry times—it keeps me on my toes.

## Critical Incident Debriefings

Let me give you an example. One dry season hit a few years ago and I wasn't sure what to do. One morning I received a call from a human resources executive representing a physician referral company. He asked me if I had a customized process developed for Anger Management that could be used for one of their doctors.

The human resources executive had been reviewing my website, and he was interested enough to call because he had seen an overview of my seminar *When Strangling Someone Isn't An Option*. As we talked I realized that my psychological training was going to play a big part in developing the proposal he was requesting. The next day I cobbled together a unique ten-hour coaching process, which include two face-to-face hours and eight hours (an hour per week) over the phone.

I realized that in order for the eight hours of phone conversation to work, I would need at least two hours for both of us to earn each other's trust and respect, face-to-face. The first two hours were a critical foundation for a successful outcome eight phone conversations later.

Here's why. Approximately 10 percent of communication is what we say, while approximately 40 percent of communication has to do with tone and voice inflection. Making up the other 50 percent is body language, which is impossible to capture over the phone.

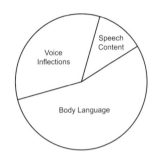

What emerged is a confidential Critical Incident Debriefing process that has now been proven effective with senior executives, other key employees, professional athletes, musicians, and entertainers. I address issues ranging from sexual harassment, rage, and racially insensitive comments to stress management, grief over the loss of a loved one, and performance enhancement in the workplace. While therapeutic dynamics are utilized, it's not therapy. It's coaching.

My point for bringing this up is that out of a dry spell came another valuable aspect of my business. I have worked with many executives and the success rate has been remarkable. Client confidentiality is one of the main keys to its success. Coaching in this manner fits my passion and helps to feed my family. Critical Incident Debriefings alone have carried us through some periods where seminars were non-existent.

Remember Lauretta? She has a passion for singing and performing. As an African American, performing Negro Spirituals is not a departure from her culture or her passion. The *reinvention* of

Lauretta is real because she has never focused specifically on this genre of music. Will she be successful at reinventing and marketing herself? Time will tell. But if I were a betting man, I'd bet the farm on her. She's hungry and this is her time to shine . . . even brighter.

---

**EXECUTIVE CONCEPTS:** Reinvention isn't something that just happens. Be on the look-out for it. Sometimes it will come to you brilliantly disguised as failure, a downturn in business, personal criticism, or hearing someone gripe about something. Try this metaphor on for size: let's say you're in the lobby of a tall building, and you have the choice between taking an elevator with one cable or an elevator with three cables. Which one would you choose? I'm right there with you on the elevator with the most cables. The same principle holds true with being an entrepreneur. It is better to have several arenas of expertise producing income streams. Diversify as much as possible without losing the intensity of your focus. If one income stream dries up for a season, look for another stream to open up and become a river.

**BONUS:** Wise investors develop high risk, medium risk and low risk strategies to make sure that their financial portfolios do not depend too much on one type of investment. Let's take a look at the game of baseball. Most baseball games are won with a single here and a double there. So it is with entrepreneurs. Not only is this an important consideration when we view our investment portfolio, but also think of the concept that time is money. Invest your time like making hits and scoring runs in a baseball game. The home run is exciting, stirring the imagination of anyone with a pulse. You've seen the historical images. The famous slugger, Babe Ruth, points to a particular part of the baseball park wall and then hits the ball over it in the general area. The place goes crazy. The hometown crowd rises to its collective feet and roars its approval. High fives are everywhere. These images transcend time. To the connoisseur of baseball, the inside-the-park homerun and the grand slam home run (four runs in at one time) are some of the more memorable sights. Just as in baseball, when it comes to business, most of us enjoy dreaming and dreaming big. But here's a word of caution: Some people are always swinging for the fences, constantly looking for the grand slam home run deal. The continual going-for–the-fence passion and perseverance is commendable. But many times they give their loved ones emotional whiplash, with all the directions they go in . . . in a decade . . . without the financial rewards to show for. They always seem to be experiencing a time, money, and/or emotional energy crisis. These folks will spend an inordinate amount of time trying to hit a grand slam at the expense of the singles and the doubles. You will not win many "games" that way. I am a "swing-for-the-fence" type of guy, and I have learned this lesson the hard way. Make sure that you apportion your time well. Make sure that you spend at least 85 to 90 percent of your business-related time hitting singles, doubles, and some triples (very hard to hit). That leaves 10 to 15 percent of your business-related time to work on the BIG DEAL—the home run! Take this advice also in terms of your investment strategy. Research carefully. Make sure that most of your money is invested in low to medium risk (secure) investments with the long term return in view. Set aside a small percentage to play with on high-risk stocks or other speculative deals. But this is the NOT the money that you are depending upon to pay next month's bills. That's called gambling!

**VISION RICH, CASH POOR:** Bring order to your life. Time is money. If you spend fifteen to twenty minutes looking for a particular item or piece of paper, think of the money that has been lost. Disorganization creates more stress, which drains a creative person of productivity. Grit your teeth and be ruthless. Throw away, or at least file papers, magazines, or other stuff that hasn't been read or handled in six months. Think of every minute saved as money in your pocket. The compelling motive behind establishing *order* is increasing *productivity* and enhancing *creativity*.

**BONUS (For Filmmakers Only):** Is filmmaking a part of your personal reinvention? Take a look at a website about an award-winning film I co-created with Don Griffin—ReturnToGlory.org—Through Edward McDougal (filmmaker and professor of film), we worked with students at a university film school. There are many film schools looking for similar projects. Below are some ideas that came out of our experience. You can view them as mere suggestions:

1. Funding—There are generally two fund-raising models:

i. For-profit model. Finding investors who are looking for a financial return on their investment. To be honest, the odds are stacked against providing a credible financial return to investors. There are many things to consider when creating your business plan for a feature film. From an investor's perspective, "bankability" is the key. You must have a "bondable" director, recognizable actors (preferably A, B+, B or C-list on the Ulmer Scale), a good distributor and you must have already secured the film rights for other foreign territories. It's hard to gain the attention of credit-worthy investors because there are plenty of other medium-risk investment opportunities providing greater return without the headaches unique to high-risk world of filmmaking.

ii. Non-profit model. Finding people who are willing to donate for a film project that can help humanity in some way. For the documentary, *Return To Glory*, we chose this option. Why? Because it took the pressure off us as we considered all of the elements of the film development process, ranging from creative control over the script and distribution to the continual stress of wanting our investors to be glad that they plunked their hard-earned cash on our project. Those who donated for this film have been more than happy with the results.

2. Let's say you are embarking upon the development of a feature length film. For those considering this idea, think of it as a process, not an event.

i. Develop a 3–5 minute film first, to get a sense of your abilities. Upload it to YouTube.com and encourage every person on the planet to review it. Encourage honest feedback as a way of improving your filmmaking skills. Current TV may even air it. Check them out online—Current.tv. You may want to do a few more film shorts before proceeding to the next level.

ii. The next phase would be to create a documentary film, which can be produced for a relatively small amount of money. Develop a subject matter about which you are passionate. Make a film trailer and upload that to YouTube.com. Have it professionally manufactured and create an online store to sell copies of the DVD. (After careful research I have found the best CD/DVD manufacturing plant. Feel free to contact me, page 201.) Do film screenings at educational institutions, assisted living homes, churches and other organizations within a 150-mile radius of your home, with a Q&A time after each screening. You will sharpen your "big-picture" filmmaking skills as a result of the comments and questions encountered at those screening events.

iii. Docudrama—develop a documentary with some dramatic elements, which will give you the needed practice on script writing, acting, camera angles, lighting, music, pathos and believability.

iv. You now may be ready to achieve your objective—a full length dramatic film.

v. Two important websites: WithoutABox.com and FilmMaking.com

## Connecting the Dots:

- CIDcoach.com—An overview of the Critical Incident Debriefing process mentioned in this chapter . . . especially designed for professional athletes and senior executives.

- There are many excellent accredited online colleges and universities, with regional bricks-n-mortar locations. Go to your favorite search engine on the Internet, using search terms like "accredited online school, entrepreneurship." Hopefully this book has awakened the need within you to sharpen your business skills. Consider taking a course on entrepreneurship. You'll be glad you did.

## Entrepreneur Club Option:
## For Personal Reflection and/or Group Discussion

1. How many income streams can you produce in your field of interest, without losing your focus?

2. Take a look back on your life. Make a list of the times you've had to reinvent yourself, writing a paragraph or two about your experiences. Celebrate each reinvention and then glean the wisdom lessons from each.

3. What is the entrepreneurial passion(s) you have considered for many years and maybe even longed to do, but never acted upon it? What needs to occur to integrate that particular passion into your life as you are currently experiencing it?

4.  What are the top three priorities in your life at this time? Are you living your life in harmony with those priorities? If so, how have those priorities informed the direction of your life at this time? If not, what needs to change so that you are in sync with what you value?

5.  Is there an aspect of that entrepreneurial passion that can be brought forward and into your life now and in the future months?

6.  At times life can seem like agitated mud in a stirred-up pond. Permitting the mud to settle and the water clearing up, is something that takes time. Make a list of the unsettled, stirred-up stuff (including your fears) in your life right now, along with the anticipated amount of time for each item to clear up.

7.  If you are considering a drastic reinvention of yourself (like going back to school or changing careers), how many incremental steps can you list—moving from where you are right now to where you want to be? Attach a timeline to that list.

8.  Do a full 360 degree view around your reinvention potential by making a list of ways you can understand all of the aspects of this personal change. In the list include items like online discussion boards, visiting your local library, reading a few books/biographies on the topic, networking with people who are already in the field you want to enter or have made their own life-altering moves . . . with some personal wisdom to share, etc.

9.  Let go of the old and embrace the reinvention process . . . the new. You will flourish. There are many who have gone on before us . . .

# CHAPTER NINE

# SO, WHAT'S YOUR FEE?

*The best time to plant a tree was 20 years ago.*
*The second best time to plant a tree is today.*

African Proverb

You may have scanned the chapter titles and decided to check out this one first. I encourage you to start from the beginning.

Before discussing fees, let's develop the concept of your having an agent. You may know of someone whom we would normally call a "people person." This individual may have many connections and be willing to serve as your agent. If you desire to be a professional speaker, writer, singer, musician, entertainer, artist, or performer, listen up.

Here's my suggestion. Sit down with that person and develop a non-exclusive agreement. In other words, you are entering into an agreement with an individual that isn't binding you to only one person as your agent.

At this moment I can hear an agent or personal manager interrupting, "Freeman, I respect the right for you to have your own opinion, but how can anyone passionately represent a talented person without an exclusive contract?"

That's a fair question. I need to remind you that this book is about people starting their own entrepreneurial business on a budget. I am giving ideas for ways to succeed from the ground up.

As stated before, the time for an exclusive contract with a trusted and proven agent may come later. For instance, most larger publishers refuse to deal directly with an author. They deal only with agents. There are some venues that will deal only with registered agents. Cross that bridge when you come to it.

The reason for a non-exclusive agreement at the beginning stages of an entrepreneurial pursuit is predicated upon the thesis that no one is more excited and passionate about what you do than you. Let an agent earn his or her right to become your exclusive agent. If your agent is really doing the job, you would jump at the chance to have an exclusive agreement with him or her. Am I right? If you have found such an agent you have found a rare gem. You are blessed indeed.

Meanwhile, here's the plan: locate someone you know who will become your agent. Anything worth discussing is worth putting on paper. Write an agreement that clarifies the percentages. Depending upon how much you charge for your services, anywhere between 10 and 20 percent is worth considering as the agent's part of the actual check you receive for your services—minus the cost of travel, hotel, ground travel, and materials. A 5 percent finder's fee may be an appropriate amount to give anyone who merely opens a door for you, with you doing the negotiating.

Include a clause in the agreement that allows you to create your own way. It can read, without legalese, something like this: "If any event comes directly to me or through me, I have the option of dealing directly with the event contact person without bringing it to or through my agent." A lawyer can slap that statement around and tighten it up.

Allow me to wax philosophical: life is like a horse race. We are all jockeys looking for a horse to ride. If the jockey gets too heavy, the horse won't run. *Translation*: if no one gets greedy, the horse will run just fine and everyone will win.

You need to make sure that whoever serves as your agent is paid enough to make it worthwhile. Also, your agent needs to make sure that you taste enough of the fruit of your labor to make it worth your while.

After all, it's you, not your agent, who will have to take off your shoes and get searched at the airport on the next gig that involves air travel. It's you, not your agent, who has to sit between two sumo wrestler-like guys in the coach section for a three-hour plane ride. It's you, not your agent, who will have to knock the socks off the attendees of the conference in spite of jet lag. It's you, not your agent, who will have to eat another meal at Denny's.

Yes, it's teamwork. Everybody plays their part. But the reality is that without you there is no event and no paycheck for anyone. It is your skill that puts another quarter in the merry-go-round. Passion for your field of interest is wonderful, but it also has to put meat and potatoes on your table.

## Fees Charged

When called by an organization interested in your services you will ultimately be hit with "The Question." Sometimes it comes early on, and sometimes it comes later in the conversation when the caller has determined that you are capable of doing a world-class job for his or her organization. Ready?

"How much do you charge?"

I do not list any fees on The Freeman Institute® website. Doing so would be like trying to give a haircut over the Internet. Why? I want to provide a verbal context for my fee while talking on the telephone. Plus, I want to be able to understand what the customer wants and why they are seeking help at this time. It is important to have a credible verbal response that strikes a genuine balance between confidence and reticence. No hemming and hawing allowed.

If you are always desperate for a gig, that sense of vulnerability will be perceived as weakness by the person on the other end of the line. You will accept any amount of money they offer you and your reputation as a soft touch will precede you. People will not want to utilize your services and they may not even know why on a conscious level. The vibe coming from a desperate person repels customers.

On the flip side, perceived haughtiness regarding your fee will equally turn off potential clients. This is a delicate subject.

Even when the financial side of your life seems hopeless, learn to be cool. It takes a cast-iron stomach to handle some of the pressures when you are in the beginning stages of any entrepreneurial pursuit. I have learned that earned money always arrives on time, even if it takes ninety days to arrive. This is your chosen profession; you must learn to deal with it.

I do not mean for this to sound arrogant, but I am at a point in my life where I can choose those with whom I want to work. There are some organizations that cause my interest to rise. What kind of situation or organization would cause me to work for less than I might normally charge?

It could be an industry I have never worked in, and I want to stretch myself. It could be with a tough audience such as a bunch of construction supervisors. I envision them with folded arms, daring the presenter to say something interesting. It could be that a friend or relative works for the organization, and I want to do him or her a favor. It could be that the mission of the organization requesting my services is compelling and intriguing to me. Sometimes I just want to do it, with no logical explanation.

## A Negotiation Script Idea

If I have decided to work with an organization, there may come a moment when I realize that they can't meet my regular fee. I have a choice. I can walk away and recommend that they utilize someone else's services, or I can pursue it.

Here is what I might say if I choose the second option, in response to the question about my fee: "You are going to have to help me out. I have an agent, and within the context of our conversation thus far, I am a wee bit embarrassed by how much he charges. But I have a clause in the agreement with my agent that provides me with two options: 1. I can send you to him for the regular fee. 2. Or I can deal directly with you, which will be a savings to your organization. I am open to exercising the second option of that clause. You can deal directly with me. My agent generally charges $_____. To some that may be a normal fee. To others, it may be way out of reach. I am a trusting soul. Go back to the other key decision-makers in your organization and do the best you can. I will tell you that I recently worked with a similar company in Arizona and they paid $_____ for a similar day-long workshop experience. Perhaps you can use that as a more realistic benchmark when you go back to talk with your associates."

What's important is for you to be absolutely honest in everything you do and say.

1. You must have a signed agreement with an agent who spends time promoting your services.

2. The signed agreement must contain a clause that presents the two stated options.

3. There must be a company in Arizona that you recently worked with, paying the amount mentioned.

"But how much do you charge for a half day or for a forty-five minute presentation?"

My typical response: "Excellent question. My fee is the same for a full day or a half day. If I fly there or drive there and back, it is actually a full day (or two) out of my life. So my fee is for the day, whether you utilize my services for thirty minutes or for six hours. I will tell you that I am available, not only to provide the keynote address in the morning, but I can also do a breakout session in the afternoon, if you want. I am yours for the entire day. Take advantage of me during the time allotted. Based on the responses of past clients, I am confident that you will be happy with the results when the day is done."

Sometimes I will be more flexible with an organization that is within a sixty to ninety minute drive from my home. I love sleeping in my own bed. Knowing that I will be sleeping in my own home that night puts a big, fat smile on my face and makes me even more open to negotiating my rate to make it work for all of us.

Be careful about the integrity of your rate. Word spreads. "You got him for what? I can't believe it! He charged us $_____." Even though I ask everyone I deal with to keep my fee in confidence, I am positive that they give broad hints when someone calls for a reference. Keep reading. In a few moments, along with some additional comments in chapter 13, I will share the non-profit option that can help you retain the integrity of your fee structure.

If finances become a sticking point, volunteer some creative ideas. If it is a large amount, sometimes it helps to suggest that they can pay you a third of the amount for three months, or half up front and half next month, interest free.

Some organizations have a part of their budget set aside for hiring the speaker and another line item for materials. The cost for materials (workbooks and handouts) for all the participants can be inflated higher than normal, coupled with the lower honorarium. Everything evens out and everyone is happy.

If you are doing a long-term job for a company, receiving less cash coupled with some company stock can become quite an interesting negotiation gambit. Receiving restricted shares (with one-to-two-year legend) demonstrates that you truly believe that your services can and will create a positive change in the company's bottom line. It also gives you some extra "juice" to make sure that your service is world class.

## The Non-Profit Option

Please understand what I am about to say. Although there are some exceptions, many faith-based and non-profit organizations generally do not value what you bring to them and are often looking for the "good-brother" or "good-sister" discount. This is the main reason why I decided to develop my speaking and staff development business for the general marketplace rather than specifically for faith-based/non-profit organizations. I do not say this to belittle or disparage these organizations. I am merely telling the truth. I know, I worked in and with non-profit and faith-based organizations for eighteen years.

I am very aware of the dynamics. One person can get excited about utilizing your services, but then has to bring it before the board. There always seems to be at least one person on the board who likes to shoot things down simply because he or she has an ax to grind with the person who really likes your proposal. This can be maddening, especially if what is being offered is needed, and you have a clearly defined, tailor-made action plan.

To be fair, many non-profits are strapped financially and are doing wonderful works. That's why I am a softie when called by one of these organizations.

Truth be told, I love working with non-profits and faith-based organizations. Sometimes it takes becoming successful in the general marketplace so that one can possess the financially capability of providing local non-profits with a service for an amount well below your normal market value. That's really my point for stating what I did in the first two paragraphs of this section.

Let's say I am negotiating with a faith-based or another type of non-profit organization that I like, and I realize that the fee is going to be much lower than usual. I will sometimes ask the event coordinator to make the check out to my non-profit organization, the Freeman Institute® Foundation. Take a look at chapter 13 for more thoughts on this topic.

The profit side of your business allows you to engage in non-profit work. Make sure that the profit side is working well and everything else in the non-profit arena will fall into place. A pastor once told me, "If the business/financial aspect of the church is failing, the ministry side suffers." That sounds like real-world wisdom, doesn't it?

**EXECUTIVE CONCEPTS:** Utilizing your own non-profit organization as the vehicle for payments is a win/win scenario for a couple of reasons: 1. Everyone has a good feeling about the transaction. 2. You are able to retain the integrity of your regular fees. 3. You are raising funds for something about which you are personally passionate.

As your confidence rises, so will your fees. You need to be aware, however, of the personal price you will pay for higher fees. As your per-event fees rise, the types of organizations that can afford your services dramatically narrows. As the number of organizations who can pay your fee diminishes, you must be at the top of your game every time you make a presentation. The word will spread to the clientele that can afford to hire you.

**VISION RICH, CASH POOR:** The simple things are profound and the profound things are simple. It may sound elementary, but keep a log of EVERYTHING you spend. After four to five weeks you may see a trend. It will come like a lightning bolt, "Wow, I didn't realize that I spend so much on junk food!" After analyzing her own buying habits, one woman told me that she spent about $65 a month on chewing gum. $65 a month is $780 a year. For someone making about $20,000 a year, she was literally chewing up nearly 4 percent of her annual income! Once she received that epiphany, she had to make some sticky decisions.

## Connecting the Dots:

- MichaelSmithAndAssociates.com—My friend, Michael Smith, has developed an annual conference for agents. This conference is one of the best in America. If you are a professional speaker, musician, or entertainer, this conference will provide the resources necessary for your

agent to be an exceptionally hard and smart worker on
your behalf. It's worth the investment.

## Entrepreneur Club Option:
## For Personal Reflection and/or Group Discussion

1.  Do you know of anyone who could become your agent?
    How will you approach him or her?

2.  How comfortable are you when talking about the money
    side of things, on a scale of one to ten, with *one* being
    very comfortable, and *ten* extremely uncomfortable.
    Who generally raises the issue of the fee, you or the
    potential client? I suggest that you follow your intuition
    regarding this aspect of the discussion of your fees.

3.  What fees do you currently charge? Why? What do you
    want to charge? Why? How will you raise your fees to
    that level? Draw a line down the center of a sheet of pa-
    per. On one half, list the upside of raising your fees, and
    on the other half, list the downside of raising your fees.
    Make a decision and closely monitor the results. The
    law of diminishing returns is no respecter of persons. Be
    aware, when a nation's economy starts falling, interest in
    anything in the service industry generally falls with it.

# CHAPTER TEN

# WORK HARD, WORK SMART

*Life is hard. It's even harder if you're stupid.*

Anonymous

Someone calls and wants to get together for lunch. As you become more successful you will get a lot of calls from people who will want to meet with you. This can dramatically affect your schedule. With long-term friends and acquaintances, you can choose the cadence of such joyful get-togethers.

When a stranger calls and wants to meet you for lunch, weigh the mutual benefits of such an expenditure of your time. Be up front about your schedule. Ask a few questions to put your finger on the pulse of the caller. If you are still not sure about meeting the person, ask a pointed question, and the decision will be made for you, "Both of our schedules are pretty crazy. What can we accomplish in person that we can't accomplish over the phone? If you can give me a compelling response to that question, I will consider your request. But I happen to have about ten minutes right now, if you want to talk."

Let your sense of humor guide you, and the caller's feelings won't get hurt. But if you do not set boundaries for yourself, no one else will. Genuinely smile when you talk on the phone and mean it. (Some people even look into a mirror while they talk on the phone, just to make sure that they aren't talking with a frown.)

Sometimes I will ask the individual on the other end of the line to help keep me on schedule. "I will give you my undivided attention, but I can only talk with you until 10:45. When my time is up, would you please help me bring this plane in for a landing?" This makes the caller your ally in completing the call in a timely manner.

I know that there is no substitute for a face-to-face meeting with people. It's just that the concept of personal boundaries needs to be understood within the context of time-management. Even though much of your business will come from the genuine relationships you build over time, you have to be careful about the amount of time spent getting together, just because someone wants to meet you.

Make a list of all the people you know, along with their contact information. Make sure that you contact everyone on that list within the first six months of embarking upon your entrepreneurial pursuit. If you have already been in business longer than that, it's still not too late to expand what you are already doing by reaching out to the varied degrees of friends and acquaintances.

When you contact past acquaintances and friends, focus your complete and genuine attention on them. This is *not* about you. Let me repeat. This is *not* about you. It's about them. Catch up with them. Reminisce about common memories. During the conversation an old friend just might ask, "So what have you been up to? Tell me what you have been doing."

You now have been granted a window of opportunity to share the excitement of your new venture—casually and briefly—along with your website address for him or her to review. The website will fill in all of the rest of the information gaps about your new business. Before you know it, your friend will be brainstorming with you about some ideas on whom you need to contact to open some doors for you. If they have connections, ask them to call the people to let them know that you will be calling. When you call, you will be amazed at how new opportunities will open up for you.

Mark Twain once said, "If you're looking for friends when you need them, you're too late."

My friend George Fraser has made sense of that statement for our purposes, "85 percent of all business is done through networking, just as 85 percent of all jobs are found through networking. Meeting people and building relationships is critical!"

I couldn't agree more. Early in your business venture, getting out to local business networking luncheons will be an important foundation for future relationships. You may even want to volunteer to become an officer of the local business luncheon. As an officer, your influence will increase and people will want to get to know you. Build genuine relationships, and the business side of things will grow organically.

Here's an additional thought: if you have attended an event and have traded business cards with fourteen people, make sure that you follow up with fourteen quick emails or phone calls within the next twenty-four to forty-eight hours. You'd be amazed; very few people actually reach out in a timely manner—if at all.

# Doing Freebies

The definition of a freebie (for me) is any event that pays under a certain amount. Your amount may be different from mine. I get calls all the time to do freebies. When I first started in 1994, I did a lot of them to help establish my reputation as a professional speaker. I still do freebies. But because of my schedule, I am extremely selective.

When I did a freebie in the early days, I would ask for certain things: a letter of reference and contacts of at least three of their peers in the same industry. This is an authentic way to build your business relationships. Imagine speaking at five events. You now have five letters of endorsement and at least fifteen semi-warm contacts. That's the start of something big.

You are giving of your time to a group that can't afford to pay you. But they are also putting you in front of people who may be able to hire you. It could very well be a win/win situation.

I remember going to speak at a multicultural counseling event in 1999, held at a local university campus on a Saturday. To be honest I really didn't want to go. I was exhausted from a lot of recent travel, which probably helped to sponsor my less-than-perky attitude. I was met at the front door by the event planner. He apologized about the small attendance. There were a few vendors along the aisles of the main hallway. They gave me an out-of-the-way table to sell some of my books.

I was one of the keynote speakers. I did a great job—had the audience on the edge of their collective seat. I also attended some of the breakout sessions and learned a lot from some other speakers. I exchanged cards with a few people. I met some interesting individuals, a few with whom I am still in contact.

I recently figured out the total amount of business that came out of that freebie (with more potential business on the way). Thus far, over seventy-five thousand dollars worth of business has emerged from an event I had driven to with a semi-negative attitude. Imagine what would have happened if I had traveled there with a semi-positive attitude! I was given a blessing I really didn't deserve.

I would encourage you to always have a positive attitude when you give of your time. When you give cheerfully, you give twice: once by performing the service and twice by performing the service with such enthusiasm that the attendees will think that you are being paid big bucks for what you are doing. I guess my moral authority to pontificate has been besmirched, so in this particular case I will have to say, "Do as I say, not as I have always done."

Know this: it is rare to get high-paying events from freebies. Why? Because organizations that can't pay professional speakers very much, generally attract attendees who represent organizations that can't pay very much. It's common sense.

Sometimes I will bring up this reality in a conversation if I feel that the person I am talking with is just a bit too pushy, "But Dr. Freeman, there will be many people in attendance who just might be interested in requesting your services later on."

I do not want this to sound demeaning, but it has been my experience that the organizations paying the least are the pickiest. They will want me to jump through yet another hoop to demonstrate that I can do a stellar job for them at a freebie fee—a Cadillac job at a Ford or Chevy price. Honestly, it can be quite maddening. It is easy to develop a sour-puss attitude. But if I have decided to do something for them, I choose to joyfully provide all the information, material, and references they require.

On the other hand, the organizations paying my regular rate generally make a decision without drama. They are very professional, with the entire booking process and logistical set up running smoothly.

If I make a decision to speak somewhere for a very low fee, it's because I am compelled and moved by the sacrifice and dedication exhibited by the participants. I generally ask them to donate some amount of money to my non-profit, because I believe that giving with some type of remuneration is important for everyone concerned. There are good feelings all around. For the most part, people will tend to respect the service for which they have paid.

Guilt, desperation, and pity have never been great motivators for me. I shut down when someone is trying to book me on a "guilt trip" in order to get me to donate my services. Over the years I have learned that if I am going to donate my services, the desire to do so will come from within my own heart and mind, not from external pressure.

---

**EXECUTIVE CONCEPTS:** Are you a natural list-maker? If not, your assignment for tonight is to make a list of all that you want to accomplish tomorrow. Draw a line through every item once it has been completed the next day. This will give you a sense of accomplishment at the end of the day. Your assignment for tomorrow evening is to do the same. Keep reminding yourself to do it until it becomes a habit.

**VISION RICH, CASH POOR:** You want to develop the graphics for a 4" x 6" postcard and then print 5,000 of them to give away or mail to prospective customers. The entire project costs about

$1,500.00. You don't want to hit your credit card for this project. What to do? There is a TV show currently on one of the home and garden channels. The premise is that a homeowner wants to fix up a section of his or her home but doesn't have the money to do the job. The TV production crew helps the homeowner sort through the "junk" and they set up a yard sale or sell it at an auction trying to raise the necessary funds. It's amazing how many times the homeowner comes up with the needed cash. You just might be astonished by how much cash you can scare up by selling stuff on eBay or by having a yard sale and selling off some of the junk around your house. Once the cash is in hand, you're ready to get those postcards printed, helping to increase the demand for your entrepreneurial pursuit.

## Connecting the Dots:

- FraserNet.com—This is a great website to visit, especially if you're interested in an annual event designed specifically for entrepreneurs. I encourage you to sign up for a regular email that will give you wisdom tips on growing your business.

## Entrepreneur Club Option:
## For Personal Reflection and/or Group Discussion

1. What factors would motivate you to want to offer your services for less than you would normally charge? Write those factors down on a piece of paper and reflect upon them the next time you are asked to do a freebie.

2. Do not be motivated by guilt, financial desperation for a gig, or your need to be needed the next time someone asks you to do a freebie. What would motivate you to

step out of what you would normally do for a person or what you would normally charge for your services?

3. What kind of boundaries do you set for yourself? Are those boundaries realistic when compared to the vision you desire to fulfill?

4. Is the vision you desire to fulfill realistic when compared to the boundaries you have set for yourself?

# CHAPTER ELEVEN

# BARTERING YOUR SERVICES

*Show me a thoroughly satisfied person,*
*and I will show you a failure.*

Thomas Edison

*Do not be misled into believing that*
*somehow the world owes you a living.*

David Sarnoff

Always keep an eye open for bartering opportunities. Check with your accountant on the tax ramifications.

If, let's say, one of your children needs braces, call around to the different dentists in your area to offer one of your arenas of expertise in exchange for a mouth full of braces for your child. Are you a computer whiz? Ask if the dentist's office needs any computers fixed or upgraded in exchange for the needed dental work for your child. It might be a painting job, a staff development seminar, framed art for their waiting room, or a lawn care job. But chances are you have something of value to offer that will either discount the actual cost or will be an even trade.

At our home we needed to have our driveway paved. I called around to several of the larger paving companies in the region. I mentioned what I did and then asked them if they would consider bartering. "I will train your supervisors for one day in exchange for having my driveway paved." After nine or ten calls, one company accepted the offer.

I worked with their sixty-five supervisors during the month of February, when their work schedule was rather slow. A few months later a crew came over to pave the driveway on our property. They did a professional job. Three years later I needed to have the driveway completed as a horseshoe, along with extra parking spaces. I called again with the same request for a different seminar program. They loved what I had done for them previously, so they accepted the barter proposal the second time. Who benefited? We all did. And that's the point. Everyone must win in order for this concept to work.

I have traveled all over the world speaking to groups of politicians and business executives. In many cases I have accepted less money in exchange for an extra plane ticket so that my wife or one of my children could come with me on an international trip. In lieu of my normal fee, I will also ask if they can front load or back load the trip with three or four days in a local resort. The presentations and training have been received very well. Once again everyone walks away with good feelings about everything.

Sometimes I will pick a country and then will reach out to companies and/or the government of that country to see if there is a need for my services. A Caribbean island nation is tantalizing, especially in January or February. You never know until you ask. I have traveled to some very exotic places simply because I made the initiation. They were intrigued that a seminar presenter/corporate trainer from the USA would make himself available. Many countries cannot pay what organizations will pay in America for similar training, but things of value cannot always be measured from a monetary perspective.

Much of my international travel has been created on the barter system because I am willing to accept less money for my services. In exchange I have traveled with my wife or one of my children, which provides an extraordinary way to grow the bond with that particular family member, one-on-one. Plus I have developed many international connections, which has helped to expand the goals and objectives of my non-profit adventures.

# Family and Business

Allow me to throw something in for free. I realize that there is a ramp-up time in any new business venture. Sixty-to-eighty-hour weeks leave little time for relaxation with the family. This is a common complaint I hear from entrepreneurs and their spouses, especially during the first few years of any startup.

Struggling with the same issues, I tried to determine how to build a business in such a way that family relationships are enhanced. I haven't always been very good at it. Someone once told me, "The definition of true success is having those who know you the best, love you the most." I am very fortunate to have a family that loves me. I am a blessed man. Without that, all of the resumé/obituary-type stuff in the world is meaningless.

An international trip with one family member coming along has proven to be just one of many strategies that has worked very well for our family. Our children have traveled all over the world with me: Singapore, Iceland, Malaysia, and Sweden to name a few. They love it! Also, my wife and I have experienced marvelous vacations before or after events in some wonderful places such as Maui, Switzerland, London, Grenada, Barbados, and other exotic destinations. Just the two of us.

If you are a parent you will understand when I say that I have experienced both success and failure as a father and a husband. Over the years my family has been very understanding and gracious. Taking a family member on trips has been one relationship-building idea that I absolutely knew was perfect for my family. My point? Discover a creative way to connect with your family while you are building your entrepreneurial pursuit. Building your business and a loving connection with your family doesn't have to be a mutually-exclusive, one-or-the-other experience.

Business growth at the expense of marriage and family makes one question the definition of genuine success. Being at the top—all alone—does not appeal to me. It's good to determine the true meaning of success as it relates to you, your family, and the others who love you.

## Some More Bartering Ideas

Let's get back to the topic at hand. Here's another bartering example: I facilitated a couple of staff-development workshops for the on-air talent, sales staff, and support staff of a powerful radio station in the DC/Baltimore region.

I now have accumulated enough ads to do a very serious radio ad campaign. I am planning to facilitate a series of open registration seminars in the entire region over the next few years with radio stations that cater to business people. These events will be co-sponsored by the station, which will give even greater publicity to the events and also will help the radio station reach out to their audience.

Let me give you an example of what we could call a "hybrid barter." It's involves a service, but also includes a healthy discount on any finances given. I provided a three-day seminar program for the sales staff, mechanics, and administration for an automobile dealership. In exchange, they allowed me to lease/purchase one of their "top-of-the-line-with-leather-seats-and-power-everything" cars for such a discounted price that I was astonished by the value. It's the automobile I currently drive, and it's all paid off.

What if you did some work for the owner of a large billboard company in exchange for, let's say, six billboards advertising your goods or services for six months on mutually-agreed upon bill-board locations? You'll never know if it will work until you call a few billboard companies and pitch the idea. It might take all of sixty to ninety minutes of your time to ferret out the viability of this kind of a barter situation. If you get some nibbles, keep pursuing the idea. No nibbles? Another blind alley. Pursue something else and chalk it up to experience.

Nothing ventured, nothing gained. Throw mud at the wall and see if anything sticks. If nothing's happening, make it happen. No pain, no gain. Okay, I'll stop. I think that I have hit the "cliché quota" for this chapter, wouldn't you agree?

---

**EXECUTIVE CONCEPTS:** The value you place on the services you provide will determine the confidence level you have when it comes to bartering. But always look first for ways you can help other organizations win. If they win, you will win. You might be amazed by how many companies will be open to working with you on a win/win scenario. But they don't have the time or the interest in such an exchange until you inform them of the concept.

You are the one who needs to create the demand for what you do by demonstrating a reasoned approach to the wild and wonderful world of bartering.

Sometimes you have to think for company owners who initially may not have a warm response to your idea. Anticipate the negative responses and build a plausible bridge to a mutually positive conclusion.

**VISION RICH, CASH POOR:** Save some money every month. Don't plunk it in the bank for the 1 to 2 percent interest. Take a look around and begin to invest it, using the "Rule of 72." But do your homework first. Go to your favorite search engine and many examples and online calculators will help you understand the ins and outs of this intriguing rule. Compound interest has the power to turn seemingly insignificant amounts into large fortunes if given enough time and invested at the right rate of return. The so-called Rule of 72 allows the investor to answer two questions:

a. How long will it take me to double my money if I earn X percent, Y percent, or Z percent?

b. What return must I earn if I wish to double my money in X number of years?

An investor who knows she can earn 15 percent on her money may ask the question, "But how long will it take to double my money at this rate of return?" Using the handy-dandy Rule of 72, this is a snap to calculate! Simply divide the magic number, 72, by the investor's rate of return, 15. The answer 4.8 is the approximate number of years it would take to double the investment. For instance, using this rule a teenager can determine when he or she wants to "retire" and travel the world. Here's an example, with approximate investment values at maturity:

$10,000 invested at 5% interest over 30 years = $43,219 investment value at maturity.

$10,000 invested at 10% interest over 30 years = $174,494 investment value at maturity.

$10,000 invested at 15% interest over 30 years = $662,118 investment value at maturity.

$10,000 invested at 20% interest over 30 years = $2,373,763 investment value at maturity.

## Connecting the Dots:

- TripsWithDad.com—I promised my four children (David, Jacob, Jesse, Shari) that each of them could go anywhere in the world with dad, when they each turned fifteen. The trips included United Kingdom, Israel, Egypt, Italy, France, Monaco, The Vatican, Hawaii, Australia, and Barbados. This website provides an overview of the "before, during, and after" benefits of such trips. If you have no small children—grown children, nephews, nieces, or grandchildren will fill the bill. It's just another way to leave a living legacy. If anywhere in the world seems too ambitious to you, why not anywhere in the hemisphere?

- Kiva.org—One of a number of microfinance options allowing you and me to have a big impact with a small amount of money. It's not quite a bartering situation, but the win/win outcome is rewarding. It's just that our win (the satisfaction of helping another human being) far outweighs the money loaned or given. If you have twenty-five dollars or more to lend, you can point and click and become part of a global village promoting sustainable development. Someone in North America, for instance, can partner with an expert seamstress or a bicycle repair person in countries like Kenya, Mexico, or Ecuador to financially launch a tailor enterprise or a bicycle repair shop. What a great feeling!

## Entrepreneur Club Option:
## For Personal Reflection and/or Group Discussion

1. What goods or services can you leverage into a win/win bartering situation?

2. Who in your geographical region can benefit from your goods or services?

3. Who internationally can benefit from your goods or services?

4. How can a win/win situation develop?

5. How will they know about this win/win situation unless you tell them? How can you create the demand for what you have to offer?

# CHAPTER TWELVE

# THE CURIOSITY-DRIVEN LIFE

*Age doesn't always bring wisdom. Sometimes age comes alone.*

Anonymous

"I will not work with idiots ever again." I scrawled that state-ment in my business diary using a red marker on Saturday morn-ing, May 15, 1993. That was a crazy time in my life. Even as I write this, several faces appear in my mind's eye. *I guess it's closer to the surface than I thought.*

I won't tell the story that led up to that particular statement. It's far too personal. But I will tell you this much. It was excru-ciatingly painful. As I remember, the previous night (May 14, 1993) was spent tossing and turning in bed. Obsessing. Analyzing. Questioning. I was evaluating everything about my life.

As I look back, I'd never want to go through that type of situ-ation again, but I view it with an appropriate awe. It was a healthy expenditure of my time and energy. That experience has informed my way of thinking and living in many tangible and intangible ways. A couple of the books I have written contain elements of wisdom I learned from that experience.

Danish existentialist Soren Kierkegaard once said, "Life is lived forward, but understood backwards." I tend to agree. Life can be interpreted once it has been experienced. Even though some challenging situations defy comprehension, the past tends to inform our understanding and grasp of the present and the future.

I am reminded of King David's (ancient Israel) rear-view look, "It was good for me that I was afflicted. . . ." One cannot be sure of which incident he was referring to, but an awakening had emerged in his consciousness that caused him to appreciate the way things were turning out and the maturity he was experiencing as a direct result of the wisdom lessons he had learned. He seemed to be aware that the "affliction" was necessary. It forced him to grow up.

When David was up to his tail in alligators, he was exclaiming, "Feet, don't fail me now! Get me away from this pain!" But later on he had developed a more philosophical view of the hard times. Panic and resentment were replaced by a respect for the various seasons of life, along with a profound gratitude to his Creator for the good, the bad, and even the ugly.

Perhaps you can relate. Life will flip you on your head, challenging you to find out if you want what you really think you want in your entrepreneurial pursuit. Be careful what you wish for and work toward. You just might get it.

Change is the one thing that never seems to change. Perhaps you have one or two tough times that have invited you to confront character flaws that were holding you back from success.

## The Brevity of Life

Caution: most challenging situations involve people. These are people that you have allowed into your circle of trust. Go forward with or without the associate(s) involved. Life is too short to waste your creative energy on hatred, bitterness, or plotting for revenge. Apologize for anything you need to address. Forgive. St. Augustine said, "Resentment is like taking poison and hoping the other person dies."

Gain perspective. I attended a wedding recently. During the ceremony the minister mentioned something I had never considered before. He said that we all need to experience the three following events at least once a year:

- celebrate the birth of a child.

- celebrate the union of two people at a wedding.

- mourn the loss of life at a funeral.

Happiness and depression never mix. Joy and sorrow mix all the time. Each experience reintroduces us to the reality that the circle of life involves birth, relationships, death, and so much more. I have never heard of a business person on his or her death bed reflecting, "I wish I had spent more time at the office."

Our schedules can get crazily busy. Just in case we have forgotten . . . some things are more important than others. I need to be reminded of that reality every once in a while, don't you?

The way to awaken this outlook on a personal level is to arbitrarily pick an age, like 90 years. Spend the next 240 seconds calculating how many years, months, weeks, days, and seconds are left on your human clock. I am currently 52 years of age. If my math is correct, this would mean that I have 38 years, which is 456 months, which is 1,976 weeks, which is 13,528 days, which is 324,672 hours, which is about 19,480,320 seconds left on earth.

This isn't a morbid exercise. Far from it! It actually slaps us in the face with the reality of our mortality, helping us live life to the fullest every minute of every day. Every moment is a gift. Inhale deeply. Exhale fully. You have just experienced a miracle.

Don't waste your sorrows; learn from them. Don't expend your energy talking negatively about others. Building up yourself and tearing down those you feel hurt you is a classic waste of time. Use that energy instead to build your own dreams and to love the ones closest to you.

# A Business Failure

A person generally does not like to talk about his failures, unless he is a professional stand-up comedian looking for new material. While building my business enterprises, I have hit a few potholes along the way.

I can remember one failure that I am still trying to figure out. One day I decided that I would provide EAP-type seminars (Employee Assistant Program), especially designed to lighten the load of human resource (HR) directors in the DC/Baltimore region. It was billed as "The HR Director's Best Friend":

**"The cost-effective alternative to self-help training, staff development, and education— enhancing relationships at work and at home. Target training. Many topics. Certificates of completion available."**

I thought that this would be at least a mild hit; an incredible resource for the smaller companies in the DC/Baltimore region that didn't have the financial horsepower to hire someone like me to do on-site staff-development seminars. I offered a cost-effective stable of world-class open-registration seminar programs on a rotating basis:

**"Dealing With People Who Drive You Crazy!"®**
*(leadership & communication skills enhancement)*

**Diversity: The Value of Mutual Respect**
*(workforce diversity and cultural awareness)*

**"When Strangling Someone Isn't An Option!"**
*(anger management & emotional intelligence)*

**"All Stressed Out and No One to Choke!"**
*(stress management and change management)*

**Succeeding in Your Organization With a Disability**
*(disability awareness)*

**"A White Man's Journey into Black History"**
*(black history and cross cultural understanding)*

But the idea went bust. Don't get me wrong. I still get calls from people who want to know when I will start implementing this idea again. Here's the open letter I placed on my website a couple of years ago. It should explain everything. As of the writing of this book, it's still there at EAPseminars.com.

Thank you for your interest. We have taken a step back from the open-registration seminars in the Baltimore/DC region. We had plenty of interest for each session, but on the day of the session only five to seven people would actually show up.

This has been a puzzle for us, because all we want to do is to offer a cost-effective way for people to attend a seminar. I have concentrated more on on-site seminar events and also individual Critical Incident Debriefings.

We'd love to bring this concept back to the Baltimore/DC region, but we are unsure how to make this program work. Any ideas?

Meanwhile, I am happy to facilitate an on-site seminar for your organization or an individual CID process. Feel free to let me know what you are thinking.

Warmest regards, Joel

We required people to pay up front and they would still not show. Our non-refundable policy ensured that they could use the payment for a future seminar offering if they could not attend the scheduled event. This became a nightmare, because then we had to offer some sort of seminar in the future, with the same low-attendance results, just to make sure that all of the people who had paid, cheerfully got their money's worth.

Even though this open registration seminar "failure" is still a puzzle, it has not been a totally wasted expenditure of our time and energy. Out of the few times we promoted these events, we met some high quality people who then brought me in to work with their organizations.

Some of the greatest connections have come through some of the greatest seeming failures. Remain alert. Failure and hard times are two things that may be used to awaken the fresh opportunities in your life.

# Motivated By Curiosity

You've heard of the *Purpose-Driven® Life*, haven't you? Well, what about the curiosity-driven life? Sometimes life gets so dark and murky that it's hard to see beyond tomorrow.

Curiosity is a powerful motivator, especially when one's vision has faded or when confusion has set in. Use it to your own advantage. Webster defines curiosity as *the desire to learn or know about anything; inquisitiveness*. Curiosity can be an important part of making it through the hard times.

What do I mean? Put yourself in any of the following scenarios:

- There is a definite down-turn in your business. Nothing that has worked in the past seems to be working now. Not even the proven . . .

- Your marriage is in trouble. Your spouse is using the "D" word and has recently mentioned . . .

- You've just discovered that your son or daughter has been experimenting with drugs in the company of . . .

- It's confusing. Your business partner is becoming unreasonable and demanding. An unusually large amount of money is missing from the . . .

- You have an unexplainable illness. Doctors have conducted every available test and don't seem to have a concrete diagnosis. You try to keep up with your business, but . . .

Any one of these situations happening in real life may cause you to hit 9.7 on the Emotional Richter Scale. Talk about an experiential earthquake! What is really happening? It's the loss of a loved one. The loss of health. The loss of a dream. The loss of an appendage. The loss of innocence. You fill in the blanks.

Grief, in any form, has to do with loss of some kind . . . which ushers in the grieving process. Loss. Denial. Anger. Bargaining. Pit of Despair. Acceptance.

Somewhere in the grieving process, a glimmer of curiosity gurgles to the surface of your consciousness. *I am intrigued. I wonder . . . how is this situation going to turn out?*

I am not sure when or where curiosity visits, but when it comes, harness it and ride it for all you can get out of it. Let it take you to another level. A fresh perspective on life.

Take a complete 360 degree view of the situation. Keep asking questions until you get solid answers. Pray. Educate yourself. Read every book on the subject you can get your hands on. Talk with wise people who will mentor you through the darkness. Listen, really listen, to them.

Start journaling. Write down every relevant thought, statement, or experience. This can be invaluable months later when you are seeking to make some sense of everything. Postmortems on tough situations don't amount to much if the relevant day-to-day thoughts and emotions aren't remembered. This might even be the catalyst for a new book, which will help thousands of readers.

A curiosity-driven person declares, "I know that things are pretty crazy at the moment but I am going to do everything I can to learn from this set of circumstances. I am curious and intrigued enough to stick around to see how everything turns out. Things can only get better. Nothing is wasted. . . ."

We pass through seasons. Winter. Spring. Summer. Fall. So it is with life. Curiosity is important at all times, whether we are experiencing a season of success or a season of seeming failure. Success is an especially challenging season because things are going well—too well in some cases for us to be motivated to even consider what's really important. We could call it *The Change Cycle* (I learned this from my friend, Sherwood Carthen, included here with his permission):

## The Change Cycle

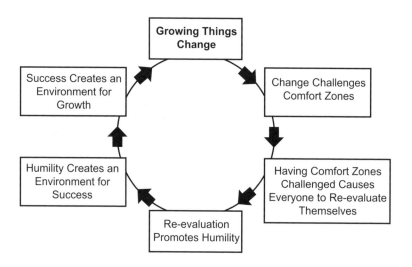

You get the picture. Every time around the circle and things are growing . . . and changing . . . and growing. Do you really want growth on every level? I believe you do. Curiosity in each stage in *The Change Cycle* permits us to squeeze every situation dry for every bit of maturity we can squeeze out of it. It's up to you to do the squeezing. It's up to God to provide the internal peace and quietness, even when the meaning of it all seems to be temporarily non-existent from our earth-bound perspective.

**EXECUTIVE CONCEPTS:** Be reminded of the people who helped you and mentored you along the way, especially your teachers and/or professors. The ones who helped you in the past may have thought they had wasted their time with you. If they are still alive, reach out to them as often as possible. Write them notes of appreciation. If you write a book, look for ways to thank them for their contributions to your life. Bring reality to the kind of dreams that will make them proud of you. I will never forget Fred and Flora Weeks—this book is dedicated to their memory. There are others, in no particular order: Arthur Freeman (my father), Katherine Freeman (my mother), Stephen Freeman (older brother), Brian Molitor, Robert Kirk (helped immensely with the refinement process of this book), Stuart Yule (best friend since 5th Grade.), Mr. Jerry Silver (teacher for both 4th and 7th Grades), Mrs. Dolsen (6th Grade teacher . . . tough, but fair), Michael Smith, Jeffrey Wright, Barry Estadt, Ivan Van Sertima, Don Griffin, Sanford Kulkin, Tom Bisset, Chuck Smith, and many more (you know who you are). My wife, Shirley, is the wind beneath my wings.

**BONUS:** Colin Powell once stated, "You have achieved excellence as a leader when people will follow you anywhere, if only out of curiosity." Can't add to that statement.

**VISION RICH, CASH POOR:** A dream without a deadline is a nightmare. I haven't always done this, but setting short-term and long-term goals, with timelines, can go a long way in developing measurable ways to check for slippage, personal laziness, blind ambition, and/or the lack of follow-through.

**BONUS (For Teenagers/Young Adults Only):** Adults aren't the only ones living curiosity-driven lives. I speak to many audiences of young adults attending educational institutions or as a part of Job Corps. When I ask for a show of hands indicating how many are interested in becoming entrepreneurs, generally between 75 and 80 percent of the hands go up. This is not surprising to me. (It's the reason why I developed a workbook, connecting the contents of this book to the next generation—NGEclubs.com.)

Angus Loten (writer for *Inc.* Magazine) stated recently, "Confirming what parents everywhere probably already know, teenagers overwhelmingly prefer being their own boss. Of more than 1,400 teens surveyed across the nation earlier this year, nearly 71 percent said they would like to run a business someday. . . . Some 32 percent said they want to start a business in professional services—the most popular industry—including law firms, insurance agencies, and accounting firms. Surprisingly, very few said the desire to own a business is driven by a lack of meaningful employment elsewhere. Instead, nearly half said they are motivated by having a great idea and wanting to see it in action."

Here are some pertinent websites, providing entrepreneurial wisdom for the next generation:

SBA.gov/teens—Small Business Administration. Excellent resource.

Titan.JA.org—The ultimate business simulation.

YouthVenture.org—A place where our next generation starts businesses.

MindPetals.com—Connecting a network of young entrepreneurs.

JA.org—Junior Achievement—Young people understanding the economics of life.

NFTE.com—National Foundation for Teaching
Entrepreneurship.
YoungEntrepreneur.com—A member-based online community.
YoungAndSuccessful.com—An online community for young
entrepreneurs.
YoungBiz.org—Empowering youth with entrepreneurial skills.

## Connecting the Dots:

- EAPseminars.com—Check out the Open Registration
seminar plan I previously described. This has been
one of my "failures." Email any ideas you think might
work. I'd love to hear from you. Perhaps I can turn the
EAP (Employee Assistance Program) Seminar program
around. I'd love to file this idea under "S" for *Success*.
Any ideas? Email: info@freemaninstitute.com

## Entrepreneur Club Option:
## For Personal Reflection and/or Group Discussion

1. Reflect on the ups and downs of your personal history.
Make a list of all the positive wisdom lessons you have
learned from these adventures.

2. Identify your biggest critics over the years. What, if anything, have you learned from them? Write a "thank you"
letter to each critic, which may help clarify any personal
lessons learned. You know the issues—you may or may
not be inclined to mail the letters. It's your decision. I
remember hearing an 88-year-old man gently say, "I
have outlived all my critics and I have out loved all my
enemies." Some day, I'd like to be able to say something
like that, wouldn't you?

# CHAPTER THIRTEEN

# THE NON-PROFIT FACTOR

*If you are not living on the edge,
then you're taking up too much space.*

Anonymous

*What matters a thousand years from now is what really matters.*

Freemanism

The development of a non-profit organization is easier and much more attainable than you may think. It is important to have a family non-profit. It helps to build character in your children, assuming that your children are younger and available to help. Plus, it sends a genuinely wonderful message to your clients.

Even if you have no immediate family, select a particular vehicle for giving back to others. I am founder of a non-profit organization—The Freeman Institute® Foundation, which is very near and dear to my heart. Funds are raised so that I can train and provide resources for highly motivated young people in organizations that would not normally have the kind of financial horsepower to hire me to facilitate leadership training for them. Since my time is limited, some of the resources are DVDs and books. Many of the sites are in urban schools, juvenile detention centers, jails, and community-based organizations. I absolutely love utilizing history and culture as the primary gateway to educate and inspire young people— FreemanInstituteFoundation.org.

Under the umbrella of The Freeman Institute® Foundation I've included another non-profit arm that is specifically designed to provide tools that promote literacy by having my books published in other translations and foreign editions. Thus far there are twenty-eight different editions, and I am delighted. Through these editions I can be in Poland, Korea, Brazil, Singapore, Ecuador, Thailand, Romania, and other parts of the world at the same time. These ten ounce "mini-me's" do not need a passport, never grumble, never take a nap, and are always willing and able to communicate. My new goal is to help publish fifty foreign editions.

"Anonymous Donors" is another extension of The Freeman Institute® Foundation. This allows me to send small amounts of money to people without the recipient knowing the identity of the giver. It's almost too much fun! One of the unique features of this arm of the Foundation is that money cannot be solicited by people from the outside. Because if the funds were given to a specific solicited need, it would no longer be an anonymous donation. If we hear about a financial need and I am able to help, I arrange to have a money order sent to that individual, with no return address on the envelope. I get great joy knowing that someone who is in a dark period of his or her life has experienced a ray of sunshine. It is my hope that the recipient will be encouraged to keep on keeping on. I love encouraging people, don't you? Whenever possible, do it anonymously. There is ancient wisdom in not "letting the left hand know what the right hand is doing."

# Benefits of a Non-Profit

Here are just a few benefits to having your own non-profit organization:

1. A non-profit can become the vehicle for you to express the altruistic part of you and your family. Get your family involved and watch how it helps everyone who loves you understand a little better about what you do and why you do it.

2. You can exercise more control over how the money is spent. Many charities and other non-profit organizations dedicate inordinately high percentages of the funds raised toward administrative costs. It is shocking how little actually gets out to the people who really need it. You can do your part to change that.

3. Rip a page out of what we could call the "Using-Your-Talents-To-Raise-Funds" playbook. Let's say you want to speak for or work for an organization that can pay you only 10 to 20 percent of what you normally charge. Protect the integrity of your fee structure by having that excellent organization make the check out to your non-profit. Everybody is happy. In the early years of your entrepreneurial pursuit you can utilize the funds to sponsor yourself in providing a service for a school, a church, a community-based organization, or other non-profits that can't pay you one penny. That way you can give while you are still earning taxable income in the form of an honorarium from your own non-profit organization, which you have legally designed for such a purpose. Once your business is more established with steady income from the business side of your life, utilize all of the funds for a specific project you have been drooling over

but could never afford to do on the non-profit side of your life.

4. What is of interest to you? What is your purpose for being alive? Answer those simple questions and you will have an incredible impact on people both locally and globally. We can call it a "Simultaneous Vision." I believe that this is entirely possible for us as individuals. Once individual efforts are combined, the positive impact is multiplied.

> *Locally*: Your non-profit organization can adopt an inner-city or rural school that would love to tell you their needs. Perhaps your non-profit will provide incentive gifts to students who get a B or above on their report cards. Inner-city schools also need computers, books, pens, chalkboards, faculty-lounge makeovers, field trips for the students, and grass on the playing field—simple stuff. Ask the principal for ideas. Initially some inner-city school principals may be a bit stand-offish, because they have seen interested people like you disappear once the initial contact has been made and false hope has been built. Don't be put off by the apparent skepticism. Finish what you start, and you will see the principal warm up after a few follow-up visits. Perhaps you can get a few other businesses and/or faith-based organization to chime in with financial and logistical support. All it takes is for one person to get the ball rolling. You just might be surprised at how little it takes to reach kids in a tangible manner. Involve your family in implementing this dream and discover how a personal vision can become a shared vision.

*Globally*: Your non-profit can adopt a small village in a Caribbean, African, South American, Central American, or Pacific Rim country. You will receive much more than you could ever give. That's a guarantee. Connect with a local faith-based organization or community college to give your efforts a more sustained impact. I have many ideas in this realm. Contact me if you are interested in exploring this concept a little more.

My wife and I have four children. Each child occupies our hearts in a unique manner, with more than enough love to go around to everyone. Each non-profit I have had a part in developing is kind of like another child, with a distinctive kinship for each. While I am excited about the goals and objectives of The Freeman Institute®, the non-profit adventures have captured my heart in very special ways.

Most people do not want the headaches of managing the paperwork required for their annual reports to the government. If that describes you, either find an already established non-profit with an excellent track record that fits your ideals and work on their behalf or find an organization that will help you manage your non-profit. I prefer the second option. Do a search on your favorite search engine using the terms "non-profit organization management, reporting." Or use the search terms that match the country in which you reside.

---

**EXECUTIVE CONCEPTS:** Use your non-profit organization to sponsor an annual awards ceremony for student scholarships, given in the honor of unsung heroes in your community. The unsung hero (or living relative) can be present on the platform as the co-presenter of the award. Name the award after your company, which will give your company another opportunity to be recognized as a positive force in the community. This will not only raise your company's profile, but will also potentially attract other donors. The more money donated, the more you can give back to the community.

**BONUS:** What if just 10 percent of the African American churches in the United States adopted the country of Haiti? A rhetorical question, but one worth considering. Many layers would have to be addressed, ranging from the obvious economic issues to the agricultural, military, political issues, and so much more. With combined resources and focused attention, I firmly believe that Haiti could become a prime tourist destination within thirty to fifty years. Max Lucado once said, "The people who make a difference are not the ones with the credentials, but the ones with the concern." All it takes is for one concerned person to capture this vision and then ignite the imagination of key leaders around America.

**VISION RICH, CASH POOR:** If you travel a little or a lot, make sure that you receive frequent flier miles. These miles add up over time. If possible use a credit card that will give you a mile for every dollar spent. The annual fee for such cards is nothing when compared to the benefits you will receive over time. Charge everything you normally pay in cash, and then bring the balance back to a zero at the end of the month. Stay disciplined on paying off the credit card at the end of each month, using the bank's money for twenty days or more to your advantage. Your normal purchases are earning free flights.

## Connecting the Dots:

- Go to your favorite search engine using the term, "non-profit corporation, charity." Immediately you will be deluged with many inexpensive ways to establish your own non-profit organization. Ask a lot of questions and then go forward with your plans. This may very well be one of the more passionate aspects of your life.

- 501c3.org—If you reside in the United States, here is the best destination: "The Foundation Group." You will want to give them a call before you go too far looking into establishing your own non-profit organization.

## Entrepreneur Club Option:
## For Personal Reflection and/or Group Discussion

1. When it comes to giving back to the community, what is your passion? Start dreaming about it. Be bold enough to create a non-profit organization even when you aren't making much money. Watch the dream develop over time.

2. How can you connect your family and/or friends to the concept of a non-profit vision? *Hint*: Let them help you develop the mission statement, core values, etc. If they help you plan it, they will take "ownership" of the vision. And if they "own" the non-profit vision with you, they will help you take care of it. Don't rush into this. Take your time, letting everyone close to you touch it along the way.

# CHAPTER FOURTEEN

# WHO'S COVERING YOUR BLIND SPOT?

*Opinions are like armpits. Everybody has*
*two of them and they stink most of the time.*

Anonymous

Most people who start their own businesses are considered pioneers, rebels with a cause. That is what's so endearing about the many inspirational books and films about people who have come up with out-of-the-box thinking in their garages or basements. Against all odds, people like Walt Disney, Jack Johnson, Michael Dell, Thomas Edison, Carlos Findlay, Madame C. J. Walker, Steve Jobs, Bi Sheng, Richard Branson, Ellen Ochoa, Booker T. Washington, Phil Knight, Bill Gates, and others have not only survived, but have gone on to become cultural/historical icons. What was accomplished in obscurity has now become common knowledge.

But during the startup stages, pioneers hear voices. "You can't do that!" "It's never been done before." "It's just not possible." "Who do you think you are?" "Haven't you failed the past fifty times you tried something like that?" "Get off your ego trip!" "Get a real job." "Wake up and smell the coffee!"

We all read later in their biographies that it was those types of statements that helped to motivate them to achieve the "impossible." It was like waving a red flag in front of a bull. "Charge!"

I could be wrong about this, but it seems like 5 percent of the people develop the business ideas and structures that supply jobs for the other 95 percent of the population. If that is true, those who would be considered a part of the 5 percent may live lonely lives, at least at the beginning of their venture(s). After success has occurred, they then have to be careful about the motives of the people who want to become their friends.

## Friends, Acquaintances, and Criticism

Criticism and negativity can be overbearing to someone embarking on an entrepreneurial pursuit. More than one dream has been shot down by a snide remark or two, an inordinate amount of sarcasm, or passive aggressive behavior from a trusted co-worker/friend.

Show me your friends and I'll show you your future. This is especially true of teenagers.

If you have acquaintances that pull you down, you will not have to actively get rid of them. They will slowly fall away if you have a purpose greater than hanging out and tearing other people down. Your vision and drive for personal and professional development will cause them to not want to be around you. In the end you will benefit. I hope that this book has sparked your interest in reaching out to others who share similar interests.

There is a thin line between listening to criticism and ignoring it. And you have to walk that line. There's no way around it. It is especially difficult when the negativity about your vision comes from someone who loves you—a best friend, an uncle, a grandparent, a brother, a sister, a parent, or your spouse.

One person can say something negative and it's like water off a duck's back. Another person can make the same statement and it makes you re-evaluate what you are doing and why you are doing it. It has a lot to do with your perspective regarding the credibility of the one making the statement. No one can make you feel inferior without your consent.

When you are flying high with a creative idea, it is important that you invite at least one trustworthy person into your life to tell you the truth. I use the word *invite* very carefully because it is incumbent upon you to make the initiation and really mean it.

# 360 Degree Vision

Right now you are reading this book. Humor me for a moment. Lift your head and look straight ahead. Put both arms up in front of you, with elbows pointed forward and your open hands up at eye level. Move them apart to the right and to the left, stopping when your hands get out of your immediate focus. There is probably about eighty degrees between your hands. Let's add thirty-five degrees on both sides to account for peripheral vision. That adds up to about 150 degrees of sight.

The 210 degrees behind you is called a blind spot. Others can clearly see what you cannot see. So it is with entrepreneurial vision. Your spouse, your family, and your customers can clearly see your vulnerabilities. Some will tell you what they see in the 210 degree zone and others won't.

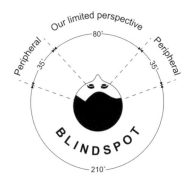

It begs the question: Who have you invited into your life, both personally and professionally, to cover the other 210 degrees behind you? This is a decision that must come from within you. You are the one who must identify at least one person to whom you give the permission to speak the truth to you.

It has been said that it is hard to read the label on a package when trying to read it from the inside. This is true of individuals and organizations.

# The Kite Story

When entrepreneurs are flying high, they need an objective perspective from a trusted friend or two. I am reminded of a little story, originally conceived by John Newton (writer of the song, *Amazing Grace*) in the late 1700s:

> The kite was flying so high that he could see for miles. This day was not like the other days, though. He was getting bored with the same view of the tall buildings, the trees, and the park. He became frustrated and wanted his freedom.
>
> The kite looked at the string and began to think, *This string is holding me back. I can't explore. I can't do my own thing.*

*I can't do the things that fulfill me and make me happy. In fact, I can't do anything I want to do myself. This is ridiculous. I'm not going to take this anymore. I think I'll cut myself free.*

So the kite did just that.

He cut the string.

He crashed.

Moral of this little story: you are the kite. You have been designed to fly high. You also have some string, some restraints in your life. Many high fliers get claustrophobic whenever they feel the restriction of rules, regulations, waiting, suffering, perceived foolishness from a business partner, emotionally-draining drama, and the need for teamwork. Makes 'em want to bust out to experience freedom once again.

But string is important. String is necessary. It keeps you grounded, while flying high. Without the string the vision dies.

The string attached to the kite represents the tension of certain important relationships, along with the legitimate rules and protocol; at the same time you can use the winds, the problems that blow against you, to fly high. Without a sufficient amount of wind the dream dies.

Every bone and tissue in your body will want to cut the string. The moment you cut the string, though, you crash and burn.

No string; no wind; no fulfillment of dreams.

Well, we have now arrived at the end of this book. But it is just the beginning of something new for you. I am truly honored that you made it this far. I have not held back. You know it's true. I have been vulnerable; disclosing a whole lot more of my life and business secrets than I initially thought I would. I have shared entrepreneurial wisdom—freely. Please do the same for others in your sphere of influence.

What have you received from this book-reading experience?

- A well-placed kick in the rear end?

- A few semi-bright ideas that have re-oriented your thinking?

- The enhanced realization that you now have some extra skills and tools for succeeding beyond your wildest imagination?

- All of the above?

It is my hope that you got what you came for. Have fun, especially when the fog rolls in. . . .

---

**EXECUTIVE CONCEPTS:** Making a tough business decision may involve soliciting advice from a trusted friend or acquaintance. Be an active listener. Take notes and review every point with a few others who love you. Carefully weigh what you are hearing. Make a decision. Be mature about the results—whether good or bad. Time will tell. If it turns out to be a bad decision, don't blame. Take personal responsibility. Chalk it up to another blind alley. If it turns out to be a good decision, shut up. Don't brag.

**BONUS:** Selective amnesia is as predictable as the law of gravity. Always, always, put a business agreement in writing—especially with a friend. It doesn't matter if your business partnership meets with success or failure. Weird things happen when two people experience low levels of trust, emotional safety, and mutual respect. Anticipate the worst-case scenarios and cover them within your agreement, including your clearly understood expectations on who is going to do what. Include the percentage received by the one who does the lion's share of the work. Add a section that allows for mediation or arbitration, instead of lawsuits. And then both of you sign it and date it, with witnesses to both signatures.

A signed document is as good as the integrity and character of the signers. Whether your business sizzles or fizzles, putting your words in writing will clarify everything. If the stakes for your venture are high, involving a trusted lawyer is probably a good option to consider.

*A word of wisdom:* If you are considering a business partnership, discuss ALL of your present and future hopes, fears and concerns. If you have to tiptoe around or not mention certain sensitive topics during the very beginning of your business relationship, it will only get worse over time. Don't rush into anything. Take your time. Put all your cards out on the table. And if you are married, trust your spouse's intuition about any potential business partners.

**VISION RICH, CASH POOR:** It doesn't cost you a penny to have a blast at what you do and how you do it. Start every day with a spring in your step. If you have adequately spread the word about your goods or services and have always delivered excellent customer service, you never know what the next telephone call or email will bring your way. People like to be around upbeat, positive people. Customers are more likely to buy from you if they like you. The fun you are having is contagious. I remember going through a stressful period in my life a couple of decades ago when I felt like a machine. "Put in a quarter and I'll dispense some advice. Put in another quarter and I'll give permission. Another quarter and you'll get a piece of my mind." Years ago I confided my mental and emotional state to Chuck Cusic, a friend of mine, who was an executive at a regional bank. He said, "Joel, I can only speak out of my own experience. When I have felt like you are feeling now, I have discovered that I was taking myself too seriously." I nodded in agreement and then he added, "Your job is legal, moral, and ethical. Work hard and take your vocation seriously, but don't take yourself seriously. Learn to laugh at yourself." This advice may not be the guarantee of your entrepreneurial success, but consciously implementing this kind of a positive attitude just may attract the kind of business success that's worth experiencing.

## Connecting the Dots:

- 360wisdom.com—This website describes the value of having one's blind spots covered through the personal/executive coaching process.

- Youth-Business.org—Youth Business International educates and then covers the blind spots of many young entrepreneurs. Already, over fourteen thousand disadvantaged young people around the world have already been set up in business. The Canadian Youth Business Foundation has developed a successful template that has other countries wanting to learn more—www.CYBF.ca.

# Entrepreneur Club Option:
## For Personal Reflection and/or Group Discussion

1. If you are a kite, who is holding your string, helping to keep you grounded? Describe your relationships with the "string-holders" in your life. Are there any changes you need to make in your attitude toward them?

2. Is there at least one person with whom you feel comfortable enough to ask to be an objective mentor to you? If so, invite him or her to give you the "unvarnished" truth at all times. Bounce unformed ideas and ask for any cautionary thoughts or words of wisdom.

3. Your assignment, if you choose to accept it: write a brief response to your experience while reading this book. Title it, "How this book has changed or enhanced my perspective on life." I'd love to read it. Feel free to email it to me.

4. If this book had a positive impact on you, consider telling at least three people about your reading experience.

5. Let's join Lauretta Young in saying, "If nobody loves you, create the demand!" Now . . . how are you and Lauretta going to put all this into action in your respective entrepreneurial pursuits?

# ENHANCING YOUR PERSONAL SUCCESS IN 30 DAYS:
## SELF-COACHING QUESTIONS

Wrestle with each of these questions over the next thirty days, writing the answers to each on a separate pad of paper. It's worth the struggle. Pause and reflect on each question even if it doesn't seem to apply to your life right now. You'll get out of it what you put in. When you have a plan, experience the difference a month can make! Many readers of the first edition of this book stated that once they finished the questions below, they read this book again with a new perspective. Not a suggestion. Just reporting . . .

## Day One

1. What contributes most to your current life success? What part does gratitude play in your daily thoughts and actions?

2. What, if anything, is holding you back in your life? How do you know this to be true and how are you going to deal with it?

## Day Two:

3. What are your weakest job skills? How do you know this to be true?

4. What are your strongest job skills? How do you know this to be true?

## Day Three:

5. Career wise, where can you go from here? What are your options? Which option is the most viable? How will you get there?

6. What would your closest friend say are your hidden talents? (Take a guess.)

## Day Four:

7. At a core level of yourself (soul) what are you trying to accomplish in your life?

8. What resides in the realm of your "shadow" (things you are trying to hide from yourself and others)? It has been said that to be alive is to be addicted in some way(s). If this is true, what are your socially-acceptable and socially-unacceptable addictions or habits and how life-controlling are they? In what specific ways? How much money do the addictions or habits you listed cost you on a daily, week, monthly, annual basis? Write those numbers down and reflect upon your response.

# Day Five:

9. What is the most influential book you have ever read? List the ways that book changed your perspective on life and send a "thank you" note to the author if he or she is still alive.

10. Are you happy with your current lifestyle? Why or why not? What, if anything, have you determined needs to change?

# Day Six:

11. Are you happy with your current family situation? Why or why not? If you are happy, how do you express your appreciation to those who love you? If you are unhappy, what will you do to change the situation?

12. What is your current spiritual practice, and is it satisfying? Why or why not? If it is satisfying, how do others around you know? If it isn't satisfying, what steps will you take to change the situation?

# Day Seven:

13. What do you do to renew and regenerate yourself? How often do you do this? List three ways (even if small ones) in which you can create and use leisure time in your life right now.

14. What is your vision of yourself in five to ten years from now? Why is this your particular vision? How will you achieve it?

## Day Eight:

15. Other than your spouse, who is your closest friend and how long have you been friends? How often do you interact with him or her and in what ways does your friend positively impact you? In what ways do you positively impact your friend?

16. What did people used to say you could be?

## Day Nine:

17. If you had to follow some other line of work, what might it be? What is it about this line of work that would draw you? What are the barriers to following that type of work? Is it worth it to you to put your effort and passion into smashing through those barriers?

18. If you have ever had a peak experience, what was it and how has it positively impacted your life?

## Day Ten:

19. Who in your family are you least alike? List the attributes and how this has affected you.

20. Who in your family are you the most alike? List the attributes and how this has affected you.

## Day Eleven:

21. Name two things that repel you. Why? How do these things affect your life?

22. Name two things you are strongly attracted to. Why? How do these things affect your life?

## Day Twelve:

23. Have there ever been any unexplainable events in your life? Name them, expressing their impact upon you.

24. Name something that energizes you. In what way(s)? And when was the last time you experienced it?

## Day Thirteen:

25. Name three things that depress or discourage you. Why? How do these things affect your life?

26. List two ideas that excite and motivate you. Why? How much energy have you put into these ideas?

## Day Fourteen:

27. What is the happiest time you can remember in your life? How has this time informed the way you currently live your life?

28. If you were required to become another living person, who might it be? Why this person?

## Day Fifteen:

29. What can you do well with the least effort and what can you do well with the most effort? How do you know?

30. The way you manage money can make the difference over time between being able to retire earlier or being able to launch into a new business venture. How well do you budget your money and then follow your budget? How often do you monitor "leaking cash" (unnecessary service fees, banking fees, credit card fees/interest and carrying debt, paying minimum monthly fees—the "cash-drains" that add up over time)?

## Day Sixteen:

31. What can you probably never do well? How comfortable are you with this knowledge?

32. Can you think of any life lessons you have avoided learning? List them. How important is it for you to learn these particular life lessons?

## Day Seventeen:

33. What is your strongest point as a person? How do you know and when did you discover this?

34. What is your weakest point as a person? How do you know and when did you discover this?

## Day Eighteen:

35. How are you unlike most people you know? How did this awareness come about?

36. Give an example of intuition in your life. List two ways this has it helped you avoid trouble?

## Day Nineteen:

37. What is the best piece of "luck" you have ever had? What are the connectors, if any, with that piece of "luck" and any of your past successes or failures?

38. What is your greatest fear? How do you know and when does it affect your life?

## Day Twenty:

39. When are you most likely to react with anger? How do others know when you are angry and how do they react? What are the assets and liabilities of expressing your anger? Make of list of both items.

40. What kind of work is play for you? When was the last time you experienced this?

## Day Twenty-One:

41. If you could live for another hundred years, what would you do with the time allotted? If you believe in an afterlife, how does that knowledge affect your present decisions and priorities?

42. Is there unforgiveness or bitterness you harbor toward anyone? If so, in what ways has it controlled or altered your life? What can you do, if anything, to resolve this?

## Day Twenty-Two:

43. What part of your life would you like to change or relive? Why?

44. Beyond career or material success, what is the core purpose of your life? How would anyone else know?

## Day Twenty-Three:

45. What does it mean to be a person of wisdom? Are you such a person? How do you know?

46. Are you content with whom or what you are becoming? By the way, who or what are you becoming? How would your best friend respond to the same question about you?

## Day Twenty-Four:

47. If a casual observer were to observe the way you live your life, what would he or she deduce your definition of success to be? On a scale of 1 to 10 (10 = extremely satisfied) how comfortable are you with this definition?

48. How will you know when you've achieved success in your life?

## Day Twenty-Five:

49. Is there anything you want to change about your criteria for success and what it is you are striving for? What will you do about this? When?

50. What do you believe about people in general? How does your behavior reveal this general belief about people?

## Day Twenty-Six:

51. What gives you hope for the future when things seem to go wrong in your work, your relationships, or in the world at large?

52. Where do you put your faith, and where would one deduce you put your faith if one were to observe the way you live your life?

## Day Twenty-Seven:

53. Does your family recognize the authenticity of your life? In what measurable ways?

54. What is the next book you are going to read? Why that particular book?

## Day Twenty-Eight:

55. Do you have a quiet center to your life? What does it mean to have a quiet center?

56. Is integrity in the small matters built into your reflexes? How are you aware of this? When was the last time you caught yourself living with integrity . . . with no one watching?

## Day Twenty-Nine:

57. Describe yourself in seven words. What image do these words portray about you?

58. Name three to five of the most influential people in your life. In what areas and in what ways did they mentor or influence you?

## Day Thirty:

59. Write a brief sketch of the remainder of your life. List at least fifteen things you want to accomplish before you die. Carry that list in your wallet, checking off items as you accomplish them.

60. What actions do you now need to take based on your responses to the previous thirty days of self-coaching questions? Make a list in order of importance. Set deadlines and cross off items as you achieve them. If you miss a deadline, reset it and try again. Don't quit!

## Day Thirty-One:

BONUS: What is the toughest question you have ever been asked? How did you respond to it at the time? How would you respond to that same question now?

# SWOT* ANALYSIS

Exploring your entrepreneurial pursuit from the perspective of: **S**trengths, **W**eaknesses, **O**pportunities, and **T**hreats

Carrying out the following analysis will often be illuminating—both in terms of pointing out what needs to be done, and in putting problems into perspective.

## Simple Rules For an Effective SWOT Analysis

1. Be honest and realistic about your strengths and weaknesses.

2. This is your perspective. It's subjective. Don't go overboard with this. Avoid over-analysis. Use it as a guide, not a prescription.

3. Avoid fuzziness. Be clear and specific.

4. This analysis should distinguish between where you are today and where you could be, or hope to be, in the future.

5. Above all, the "KISS Principle" is in order. Keep it short and simple.

| **S**trengths: (Build on Them) | **W**eaknesses: (Resolve Them) |
|---|---|
| What are your advantages? | What could be improved? |
| What do you do well? | What do you do badly? |
| Why did you decide to enter the field you did? | What should you avoid? |
| What were the motivating factors and influences? | What do you do poorly or not at all? |
| What relevant resources do you have? | What objections do potential clients frequently raise? |
| What do other people see as your strengths? | What are your professional weaknesses? |
| Do these factors still represent some of your inherent strengths? | How do these weaknesses affect your job performance? (These might include weakness in technical skill areas or in leadership or interpersonal skills.) |
| What need do you expect to fill within your organization? | |
| What have been your most notable achievements? | Think about your most unpleasant experiences in school or in past jobs, and consider whether some aspect of your personal or professional life could be a root cause. |
| To what do you attribute your success? | |
| How do you measure your success? | |
| What knowledge or expertise will you bring to the company you join that may not have been available to the organization before? | NOTE: Consider this from an internal and external basis. Do other people seem to perceive weaknesses that you do not see? It is best to be realistic now, and face any unpleasant truths as soon as possible. |
| What is your greatest asset? | |
| NOTE: Consider this from your own point of view and from the point of view of the people you deal with. Don't be modest—be realistic. If you are having any difficulty with this, try writing down a list of your characteristics. Some of these will hopefully be strengths! | |

*(Left margin vertical label: INTERNAL FACTORS)*

| **O**pportunities: (Exploit Them) | **T**hreats: (Avoid Them) |
|---|---|
| What are the promising prospects facing you? | What threatens the current personal & organizational growth? |
| What are the best opportunities in the near future? | What obstacles do you face? |
| What is the "state of the art" in your particular area of expertise? | Are the requirements for your desired job field changing? |
| Are you doing everything you can to enhance your exposure to this area? | Could any of your weaknesses seriously threaten your business? |
| What formal training and education can you add to your credentials that might position you appropriately for more opportunities? | Who is your competition and what are they doing well? |
| Would an MBA or another graduate degree add to your advantage? | Does changing technology threaten your prospective position? |
| How quickly are you likely to advance in your chosen career? | What is the current trend line for your personal area of expertise? |
| List changes in government policy related to your field? | Could your area of interest be fading in comparison to more emergent fields? |
| What are the interesting trends: such as changes in social patterns, media, technology (macro/micro), economy, population profiles, lifestyle changes, etc.? | Is there a bad debt or cash flow problem? |
|  | Is your chosen field subject to internal politics that will lead to conflict? |
|  | Is there any way to change the politics or to defuse your involvement in potential disputes? |
| NOTE: One useful approach when looking at opportunities is to look at your strengths and ask yourself whether these open up any opportunities. Alternatively, look at your weaknesses and ask yourself whether you could open up opportunities by eliminating them. | How might the economy negatively affect your future company and your work group? |
|  | Will your future company provide enough access to new challenges to keep you sharp—and marketable—in the event of sudden unemployment? |

(Left margin vertical label: EXTERNAL FACTORS)

* The creator of the SWOT method is not known, but it is a technique that became popular for business strategic planning in the 1960s, and then was adapted for broader use in many other fields where strategic planning was needed.

# IF I CAN WRITE, YOU CAN WRITE

*Always remember that you're unique. Just like everybody else.*

Anonymous

**1.** When you write your autobiography, **start by dividing your life into decades**: birth to ten years old, eleven to twenty years old, twenty-one to thirty, thirty-one to forty, and so on. Think carefully about each decade; identify the many different experiences in each decade: the highs and the lows, the funny and the serious, the boring and the exciting. You get the picture. Take the time to write about each experience. Fill in the gaps. Try to remember what you were wearing, the weather, your emotional state, the interior and exterior colors of your childhood home(s), the pictures on the walls, and the people involved. For the early years ask your parents, siblings, relatives, neighbors, and friends to try to help you by sharing their memories of you. Do it soon. Some of your more elderly relatives may not be around when you get serious about it. Get out your video camera on a Sunday afternoon and ask them all sorts of questions about your family history. Plan it in your schedule right away. This is not only a valuable legacy you are passing on to the next generation, but it will be an invaluable way to provide fodder for your own autobiography when you get around to writing it. Start planning for your autobiography now, regardless how you feel about your life right now. Live the kind of life that causes people to expect an autobiography from you. "So when will you be writing your life story?"

Here's the formula: Select the most dramatic moment of your life. Start the book with a cliffhanger, grabbing the reader with the energy of that pulse-pounding event. "The brilliance of the sunset was blinding as I scanned the horizon. *She should've been here by now.* With night approaching, the surrounding scene before me brought nothing but despair and desolation. Blam! Stunned, I turned my head. . . ."

What was the "blam" all about? Who is the woman? What was I about to see when I turned my head? Grab the attention within the first few sentences. End the first chapter—but don't quite give full closure to the drama yet—with something like "but it wasn't always that way. . . ." Now with chapter two and beyond, you can go back to your childhood, weaving in bits of pithy advice as you write. Later on in the book, you can bring some sense of closure to the events in the first chapter. Give the reader a reason for wanting to read more. Tease and then deliver with more than the reader could have ever expected.

**2. Think of perhaps ten to twelve wisdom lessons** such as: "Never, never, never give up," "Don't be afraid to say *I'm sorry,*" or "Have a mentor, be a mentor." Once you have identified ten to twelve wisdom lessons, search for stories in your life or in the life of another person that illustrate those wisdom lessons. You may remember one, two, or even three stories for each lesson. This way you can tell your life story and share wisdom principles at the same time. This gives your book an even greater life-changing quality to it. Very few autobiographies capture the general interest of readers. Unless you are enormously popular, you will have to develop your autobiography with a WIIFM perspective—"What's In It For Me?" What would motivate someone to want to read about your life?

**3. Show, don't tell.** There is a general tendency to pontificate or even "preach" about success on your chosen topic, which is absolutely boring to the average reader. Malpractice of the literary kind. Do you want to illustrate the principle of perseverance or forgiveness? Share your heart and mind through a personal encounter with bitterness or a story about Raymond or Saundra—a friend/mentor who impacted your life in a tangible manner. That way if your friend/mentor happens to use the Bible or some other source to talk about forgiveness, the reader is vicariously learning about inspirational principles through another person's experience—the power of the third party. It is much easier to learn about it that way than having you, the author, state the same thing directly to the reader.

**4. Follow every major point with an illustration.**

**5. What about the marketing value of a novel?** Novels are very hard to "sell" as a good talk-show topic. Think like a radio talk-show host and the nonfiction "hooks" will begin to emerge. Fern Reiss (author of ten bestselling books) states, "Develop a few good nonfiction hooks in your novel and then plan your marketing efforts around them. If your character is an avid golfer, you can sell your novel at golf conventions, golf shows, golf pro shops, and golf courses. If your novel focuses around golden retrievers, you can find and market to the (vast) dog-loving audience. Golfers like to read books about golfers, and dog-lovers like to read books about dogs, so be sure you're working your hooks and going after your natural audience." This is great information.

**6. Try to figure out the answers to the following questions:** A) How is my book different from all other books on the topic of _____? B) What makes me a credible author? C) Why would anyone want to read a book about _____? D) How am I willing to promote this book? These are important questions to address. Your publisher will be glad to hear that you have been thinking like this, because this is how he/she thinks. This is a business. The publisher has to sell at least five thousand copies just to break even on your book, so try to think of ways for the publisher to at least break even. Then everyone can have fun.

**7. Reasons why people purchase books:** (in order) 1) subject matter 2) author's reputation 3) price 4) religious affiliation 5) book reviews 6) cover illustrations 7) publisher (published in Bookstore Journal)

Publisher Bob Young states that over 220,000 books are published in North America every year. The chances of any book becoming a bestseller are 0.01 percent.

**8. Establish "eye contact" with reader early on.** Most people do not read a book in one setting. Remind then periodically of your purpose for the book. Keep re-establishing eye-contact periodically throughout the book. "You might be wondering. . . ." "I am so glad that you asked. . . ." "The fact that you made it this far says a lot about. . . ."

**9. Absolutely no one (publisher, publicist, etc.) is more excited about your book than you.** Budget that into the account of your mind, and remember that as you go forward in the promotion process. If your book is with a publisher, ask the telephone and traveling sales people to interview you for five to ten minutes. They are dealing with so many titles that your book is just another book. They read from the prepared promotional sheet when asking a distributor or store chain to get some of your books. Imagine a salesperson stopping mid-sentence, exclaiming to the book buyer, "You really want this book! I met the author over the phone and. . . ." Even if you are a first-time author, the buyer will be intrigued enough to order some test copies to see how it sells.

**10. Books are expensive business cards**. Very few people will actually read your book from cover to cover, but those who do will pass the word on, if it truly is a good/inspirational read. A book also will open many more doors for you to speak in other parts of the world. You will end up giving books away to key decision-makers who will bring you in to speak at conferences. Events will help you to sell books. Do whatever it takes to polish your ability to speak professionally. Why? If you do not speak, copies of your books will be stacked in your basement, attic, closets, and under your bed.

**11. Establish at least one, if not two "take-aways."** These are heart-rending, emotional stories that grip the reader's imagination. Ten years later, someone will say, "I remember that book. I remember the story you told about the time your friend's home burned down and they lost their eight-year-old son." These stories will stay with people far longer than ten positive statements to demonstrate some principle that is important to you.

**12. Determine your writing style.** Be comfortable with breaking some grammatical rules. Most people talk and think at about a sixth grade level. In fact most situation comedies on TV are geared to the twelve-year-old mind. Don't patronize, but write in a reader-friendly style that is comfortable for you. Some people may say, "I felt like I could actually hear you talking while I was reading your book."

**13. Trust the safety net of an editorial staff.** Sometimes I will slip in something controversial to see if it will slip by my editor. Trust editors when they say, "Perhaps that particular story is a bit too honest for readers." That's the type of story you can tell effectively at a conference, but shouldn't be included in a book. Most readers haven't looked into your eyes and watched the integrity of your life.

**14.** At the same time, **be as real, as honest, and as vulnerable as is prudent for you**, in the position you currently occupy. Many successful people write glossy books about the triumphant/high experiences of their lives. While reading books like that, I talk back to the writer, "I wanted to know more about you, but you kept sharing the highs. What about the lows? I am having a hard time relating to you." While you want to inspire readers, you do not want to present such a positive, upbeat picture that the average reader can't identify with you. Someone once said, "We learn from suffering, but not from prosperity." Alexander Solzhenitsyn adds, "We know that the human spirit can survive depravation, but we are not sure that it can survive success." Success is wonderful, but it is not such a good teacher—if your intent is to teach.

**15. Most readers are somewhat cynical and lazy.** (Of course, not the readers of this book!) They have very high expectations and demand excellence. Surprise them with something so different that they can't put the book down once they start reading. The first few paragraphs should hit the reader right between the eyes. Every chapter should start with something so extremely interesting that will compel the reader to keep reading until the book is finished. Write the kind of book that will bring this kind of feedback, "I started reading your book at ten o'clock at night, and I couldn't put it down! I stayed up all night reading it."

**16. People approach the purchase of a new book different-ly.** What are the "emotional triggers" you can utilize to create the desire to purchase your book? The next time you are in a bookshop set aside some time to do some research. Watch closely as people browse, stopping to take a new book off the shelf. Some will open the back first to read the notes or bibliography. They want to determine the "wells" from which the author drew his or her water. Others will read the back cover first. Some will take the time to read the promotional blurbs and endorsements. Some open the book directly to the table of contents to get a sense of the themes covered by the manuscript. Some flip it open anywhere to see if something grabs them. Different strokes for different folks. Make sure that you develop hooks for everyone. The "AIDA Process" indicates that there are four stages to a purchase. Make sure that your book provides a smooth transition between each stage:

- **A: Attention**—Something about the book grabs immediate attention (title, cover art, subtitle).

- **I: Interest**—Create interest in wanting to learn more (back cover, endorsements, author's bio, table of contents).

- **D: Desire**—Increase the desire to purchase your book (chapter content, price).

- **A: Action**—Actual purchase of the item (you have reached another person).

**17. What about a foreword for your book?** I don't like them. Most people don't even read them. They skip right over. Notice what I did in this book. I wrote a foreword, jazzed it up a bit and then made it the first chapter. I'll bet that you read it. Let me take a step back and say that I will, on occasion, utilize the well-written foreword of a respected person if it will help the reader connect with my book.

**18. Become an expert at writing dialogue.** Read some novels to see how it is done. The average novel is about 80 percent dialogue. If you are writing non-fiction, you can still spice it up with dialogue. We learn so much about people by the way they speak and when they speak. As you are reading novels, write down words used in dialogue. "He said and she said" are way too predictable and stiff. Instead try word pictures like he bellowed, she purred. Immediately you get a glimpse of the size, the mood, the attitude of the person. Write down all of the dialogue words you can find and then work many of them into your manuscript: sighed, groaned, huffed, whispered, hissed, cajoled, growled, smiled—you get the picture.

**19. The writing process is hard work**. It's boring. Plus, you can be sure that you will re-write your book several times. Commit yourself to the process, because the finished product will be wonderful. If nothing else, the writing process will tighten your presentation/speaking skills like few other disciplines. Believe in what you are writing. Set a cadence that works for you. One hour a day? Four hours a week?

**20. View your book as a little ten-ounce missionary.** As you write, consider how the book will translate into other languages. In this manner you multiply yourself a million times over. Be aware that changes will have to be made. For instance, the *trunk* of a car in the North America is a *boot* in the UK.

You can only be in one place at one time, but your life story can be in China, Poland, Brazil, US, Canada, and France reaching thousands of lives all at the same time! I refuse to take royalties for books translated into other languages. The publisher gets to keep all royalties and sales. Hopefully they will then have the financial ability to print more books. I view it as economic empowerment for a publisher, plus it permits the publisher to advance the mission he or she has been given. A book never needs life or health insurance. It never needs eight hours of sleep. It never complains and it never gets grumpy or weary of helping people. Never takes a coffee break. But it will increase literacy and change lives as long as it exists in printed form. That is a compelling and powerful thought.

Also, in some developing nations the printed word is still revered. The general population hasn't been hit yet by the confusion of five hundred or more TV channels. About fifteen years ago a Polish publisher told me that on average one book was read by about twenty-five people. I do not know if that is still true, but think about five thousand copies of your book printed in the Polish language, distributed throughout the country of Poland. If this is still true, 125,000 people will have ultimately been impacted by the first printing of your book. Let the reality of this scenario sink in.

**21. Buy the domain name of the title of your current book,** along with any other titles that are floating about in your head. Get the dot com version, since most people think "dot com." If the title of your book isn't available, get a memorable and mildly humorous domain name like JoelWritesRealGood.com. (Yes, I own that one, too!) You also may want to consider getting your own name as a domain name. I have a great place to buy domain names. They are under nine bucks a year and that includes free forwarding and masking: **MultiWebConcepts.com**. Make sure that you come up with domain names that you can give out during radio interviews. Think about catchy domain names that listeners will remember, even if they can't write it down while driving in city traffic. Make sure that the domain names you choose are easy to understand and easy to spell. If someone already has the domain name you want, get creative. Let's say you want to purchase and own publishing.com, but it is no longer available. How about these alternative ideas: 123publishing.com, publishing101.com, ABCpublishing.com, RealHotPublishing.com, GreatPublishing.com, or PrettyGoodPublishing.com. Does this make sense?

**22.** Should you self-publish or have a regular publishing house publish it? I have done both. A **publishing house** will give you prestige and market presence and will also make your book available to every library and bookstore in the country. Events sell books. On the other hand, **self-publishing** will give you complete control and the potential for more cash if you do a lot of events. If you self-publish, here is a great place to get the best pricing on printing: **PrintingForGood.com**. This company operates as a broker. It's one of the few times I have seen that using the middle man can save you money. They have access to incredibly cheap cover graphics work, pagination, and printing costs. At least give them a chance to amaze you. The Internet has changed all the rules. Just a decade ago, I would have never counseled anyone to self-publish. But times are different. It's still hard work, but the odds for success have shifted in your favor.

### 23. Negotiating a contract with a publishing house:

a) Make sure that you get a **rising royalty rate**. Let's say 15 percent for the first 15,000 copies sold, 17 percent up to 25,000 copies and then 21 percent for over 40,000 copies sold. This gives you some incentive, some numbers to shoot for. You might even want to suggest something real crazy. If you are motivated by a challenge, tell your publisher that you'd like to have a clause in your contract that states, "If this book goes over 100,000 copies author receives 25 percent of every book sold thereafter."

b) You will make the most money on **copies sold** after speaking engagements and from your online store.

A great place to develop your own bookstore is **PersonalBookstore.com**. Read the information and then click on the appropriate button (Become A Retailer) to sign up for your own store. You can sell your own book and/or music and get a percentage of the the sales of all other products through your own store. Plus they take care of all the credit card issues.

c) Do you want an **author's advance**? Good question. An advance is just that—an advance against your future royalties. The positive side is that an advance helps to drive a stake in the ground. Publishers aren't going to bump your book for another, more sexy title if the only way they can recoup their investment is to sell your book. Having said that, an advance isn't such a good idea unless it's over $50,000. If you like to speak publicly, why not get copies of your book given to you, instead of an advance? Let's say they want to give you an advance of $10,000. Sounds great, but remember that they are taking that money out of your pocket. Let's take a look at another option. What if they gave you 2,500 books instead of an advance? The actual cost to your publisher may be approximately $1.50 a book—$3,750—depending upon the print run, size, and cover. You sell the books after your speaking events and on your online store. Let's say you sell them for $15 each. You have made $37,500. And the money you have earned wasn't an advance against your future royalties. Big difference! You get royalties from the first book sold in bookstores. Here's the win/win: Your publisher has put less money out, and the time between your publisher's outlay of money and the recouping of their investment is much smaller. Everybody is happy!

d) Negotiating your **authors' copies** can be fun. They will try to get you to take a 60 percent or 65 percent discount off retail. Tell the publisher that you work from the bottom up—versus top down. This may be a tough sell, but if your manuscript is good enough you might have more negotiation muscle than you realize. If they are printing 5,000 copies on the first print run, a hundred-sixty-page book may cost them at most about $1.50, depending on a number of things (embossed cover, quality of paper, printing in Hong Kong, etc). Offer them 20 percent over the manufacturing cost at $1.80 per book, if you buy them by the case and 15 percent over the manufacturing cost if you purchase ten cases at a time. Educate them by telling them that every book you sell on the table in the back of the room will encourage the sale of two to three more copies through the bookstores.

e) Ask to have a publicist assigned to you for three to six months, so that the success of the book launch is increased. With the use of your phone you can do many radio interviews all over North America without ever leaving your home office.

f) Do you want to retain the audio book, movie, and DVD presentation rights? Are those right important enough to you to make as non-negotiable issues? How about the pocketbook rights? Be careful about exercising the pocketbook rights. The moment you exercise those rights, it will kill the sales of the larger, more expensive editions, along with your royalties from the more expensive editions. In fairness, make sure that enough time has elapsed and make sure that your publisher has some say in when the mass pocketbook edition can be released, if it is less than two to three years after the printing of the first edition. If that provision isn't included, your publisher may back off of his/her commitment to the publicity of your book.

**24. Book Title**—You can hang your book on a snappy title and then explain it with a subtitle. Let me give an example. I looked on Amazon.com a few minutes ago and typed in the first strange word that popped into my head, "Zap." I found a book called Zap. What does "Zap" mean? The subtitle said it all—"A Brief History of Television." Once I read the subtitle, the word "zap" made more sense. It's a catchy, easy to grasp concept once you hear the subtitle. You can even work a nice domain name around it—www.zapTVbook.com. Is this domain name still available? I don't know, but chances are good that it (or something like it) is still available. A book titled *A Brief History of Television* might elicit a few yawns. This is but a quick example of how you can throw away a stuffy title, replacing it with something that communicates what you want to communicate, with a bit of zip to it—if that's what you want.

**25. Book Cover**—Be very careful about "dating" the cover. Photographs can be a dead giveaway. Remember the 1970s? Wide ties, plaids, bell-bottoms, wide lapels on sports jackets, and weird sideburns on men. Disco was the rage. Imagine writing a book during that era, with a photograph of several people on the front cover. Within a few years that book would be laughable, even though the inside information of that book may be timeless. Those are the kinds of books that sit for years on the shelves of thrift stores across the country. Fast-forward to today. What's "in" right now, will not be popular within a few months or years.

Some of the latest demographic studies indicate that by the year 2050 there will be **no clear ethnic majority** in the United States. We live on a "shrinking planet." With this thought in mind, are you conscious of how potential readers from various ethnicities will respond to the images on the cover of your book? People pictured on the cover of most books are Caucasians or an image of a Caucasian hand holding something. It is important to consider your various audiences. If you really want to reach a wider audience, solicit opinions from people of other ethnicities who love you and who will speak the truth. Really listen to their perspectives. Just to be safe you may want to go with another concept, something other than people pictured on the cover. If you are a man, solicit the opinions of several women and vice versa. This kind of stuff should be common sense, but it still continues to amaze me how little some people think about the impact of the cover for audiences outside of personal "culture comfort" zones.

Additional idea: While discussing book covers—I heard somewhere that **80 percent of all books are purchased by women**. I have no reason to doubt that number. If that is true, make sure that the cover appeals to the majority of people who will be purchasing your book. If men are your primary target audience, make sure that you incorporate some elements in the cover that attract women, who will buy it for the man/men in their lives—husbands, sons, fathers, brothers, nephews, uncles, and boyfriends.

**26.** Your online store should say something like, **"Where else can you get this book autographed by the author?"** You make more when you sell the book so you need to set your online store apart from any other venue where someone can go to purchase your book.

**27.** Develop a **unique way to sign** and personalize the books you have authored. I have developed a different statement for every book I have written, but I sign them all the same way— *100,000 Blessings, Joel A. Freeman.* That's my unique signature. Figure out something that is memorable and different, fitting your personality.

# NOT JUST FOR GRAPHIC ARTISTS AND DESIGNERS

If you are an artist, painter, or graphics designer in business for yourself this list (written by Mark A. Lewis*) will mean a lot to you. For the rest of us, this unedited list will help us to have greater understanding and respect the next time we need a new logo, letterhead, or brochure designed. It was originally titled *"Top 10 Lies Told to Naïve Artists and Designers."*

### 1. "Do this one cheap (or free) and we'll make it up on the next one."

No reputable business-person would first give away their work and time or merchandise on the hope of making it up later. Can you imagine what a plumber would say if you said "come in, provide and install the sink for free, and next time we'll make it up when we need a sink." You would be laughed at! Also the likelihood is that if something important came along, they wouldn't use you.

**2. "We never pay a cent until we see the final product."**

This is a crock, unless the person is leaving the door open to cheat you out of your pay. Virtually every profession requires a deposit or incremental payment during anything but the smallest project. Once you have a working relationship, you may work out another arrangement with a client. But a new client should not ask you to go beyond an initial meeting or, perhaps some preliminary sketches, without pay on the job!

**3. "Do this for us and you'll get great exposure! The jobs will just pour in!"**

Baloney. Tell a plumber, "Install this sink and my friends will see it and you'll get lots of business!" Our plumber friend would say, "You mean even if I do a good job I have to give my work away to get noticed? Then it isn't worth the notice." Also the guy would likely brag to everyone he knows about how this would normally cost (X) dollars, but brilliant businessman that he is he got it for free! If anyone calls, they'll expect the same or better deal.

**4. On looking at sketches or concepts: "Well, we aren't sure if we want to use you yet, but leave your material here so I can talk to my partner/investor/wife/clergy."**

You can be sure that fifteen minutes after you leave he will be on the phone to other designers, now with concepts in hand, asking for price quotes. When you call back you will be informed that your prices were too high and Joe Blow Design/Illustration will be doing the job. Why shouldn't they be cheaper? You just gave them hours of free consulting work! Until you have a deal, LEAVE NOTHING CREATIVE at the client's office.

**5. "Well, the job isn't CANCELLED, just delayed. Keep the account open and we'll continue in a month or two."**

Ummm . . . probably not. If something is hot and then it's not, it could be dead. It would be a mistake to *not* bill for work performed at this point—then let the chips fall where they may. Call in two months and someone else may be in that job. And guess what? They don't know you at all.

**6. "Contract? We don't need no stinking contract! Aren't we friends?"**

Yes, we are friends, until something goes wrong or is misunderstood, then you are the jerk in the suit and I am that idiot designer. At that moment the contract is essential. That is, unless one doesn't care about being paid. Any reputable business uses paperwork to define relationships, and you should too.

**7. "Send me a bill after the work goes to press."**

Why wait for an irrelevant deadline to send an invoice? You stand behind your work, right? You are honest, right? Why would you feel bound to this deadline? Once you deliver the work and it is accepted, BILL IT. This point may just be a delaying tactic so the job goes through the printer prior to any question of your being paid. If the guy waits for the job to be printed, and you do changes as necessary, then he can stiff you and not take a chance that he'll have to pay someone else for changes.

**8. "The last guy did it for XXX dollars."**

That is irrelevant. If the last guy was so good they wouldn't be talking to you, now would they? And what that guy charged means nothing to you, really. People who charge too little for their time go out of business (or self-destruct financially, or change occupations) and then someone else has to step in. Set a fair price and stick to it.

### 9. "Our budget is XXX dollars, firm."

Amazing, isn't it? This guy goes out to buy a car and knows exactly what he is going to spend before even looking or researching it? Not likely. A certain amount of work costs a certain amount of money. If they don't have the money, you can decide do less work and still take the job. But make sure they understand that you are doing *less work* if you take *less money* than you originally estimated. Give fewer comps, simplify, let them go elsewhere for services (like films), etc.

### 10. "We are having financial problems. Give us the work, we'll make some money and we'll pay you. Simple."

Yeah, except that when the money comes, you can expect you will be pretty low on the list to be paid. If someone reaches the point of admitting that the company is in trouble, then things are probably much worse off than he or she is admitting to. Even then, are you a bank? Are you qualified to check out their financials? If the company is strapped to the point where credit is a problem with credit agencies, banks etc., what business would you have extending credit to them. You have exactly ZERO pull once they have the work. Noble intentions or not, this is probably a losing bet. But if you are going to roll the dice, AT LEAST you should be getting additional money for waiting. The bank gets interest and so should you. That is probably why the person is approaching you—to get six months worth of free interest instead of paying bank rates for credit and then paying you with that money. Don't give away money.

# AFTERTHOUGHTS

This list wasn't meant to make anyone crazy or paranoid, but is designed to inject some reality into the fantasy.

You are going to be dealing with people who are unlike yourself. Their motivations are their own and their attitudes are probably different than yours. There are going to be demands, problems, issues and all the hassles that go with any work/job/money situation. Too many times I see the sad example of someone walking into a situation with noble intentions and then getting royally screwed, because what they see as an opportunity and a labor of love, the other party sees as something else entirely, not at all romantic or idealized, but raw and simple.

How can you deal with this stuff and still do good creative work? Good question. This is why an education is important. You learn, out of the line of fire, how to deal with the art at its own level and also how to deal with the garbage that surrounds it. You may have tough teachers and think that it can't be worse, but wait until a business-person has a hundred grand riding on your art! Then you will know what "demanding" means. You will then thank all those tough teachers for building up the calluses that enable you to enjoy the job rather than just feeling like it is all a big waste of time!

In the end, working commercially, being a terrific artist is about 25 percent of the task. If that is the only part of the task that you are interested in, do yourself a favor. Don't turn "pro."

* I couldn't locate the author, Mark W. Lewis, even after an exhaustive search on the Internet. The first mention of this list on the Internet is at: JeremySutton.com/advice.html.

# WORDS WORTH EMBROIDERING

*There isn't much traffic in the Extra Mile.*

Anonymous

"Good leaders are like baseball umpires: they go practically unnoticed when they are doing their jobs right." —Byrd Baggett

"The person who is not hungry says that the coconut has a hard shell." —African Tribal Saying

"The cynic is his own worst enemy. It requires far less skill to run a wrecking company than it does to be an architect." —U.S. Andersen

"It takes a steady hand to carry a full cup." —Anonymous

"The thing I hate about an argument is that it always interrupts a good discussion." —G.K. Chesterton

"A man's mind that is stretched to a new idea never goes back to its original dimensions."—Oliver Wendell Holmes

"Failure is success if we learn from it." —Malcolm Forbes

"You miss 100 percent of the shots you never take."
—Wayne Gretzky

"A smart businessperson is one who makes a mistake, learns from it, and never makes it again. A wise businessperson is one who finds a smart business person and learns from him how to avoid the mistakes he made." —Jim Abrams

"Confidence is the hinge on the door to success."
—Mary O'Hare Dumas

"What worries you masters you." —Haddon W. Robinson

"Injustice is relatively easy to bear; what stings is justice."
—H.L. Mencken

"The optimist proclaims that we live in the best of all possible worlds; and the pessimist fears this is true." —James Clabell

"Speak in anger and you'll give the greatest speech you'll ever regret." —Anonymous

"It is not the size of the dog in the fight, it is the size of the fight in the dog!" —Anonymous

"It is useless for sheep to pass a resolution in favor of vegetarianism while wolves remain of a different opinion."
—William Randolph Inge

"Patience is the companion of wisdom." —Anonymous

"If you think nobody cares if you are alive, try missing a couple of car payments." —Earl Wilson

"The degree of one's emotion varies inversely with one's knowledge of the facts—the less you know the hotter you get."
—Bertrand Russell

"If we find a man of rare intellect, we should ask him what books he reads." —Ralph Waldo Emerson

"The company's most urgent task is to learn to welcome, beg for, demand—innovation from everyone." —Tom Peters

"Creativity is the sudden cessation of stupidity." —Dr. E. Land

"The easiest thing to find is fault." —Anonymous

"Whether you think you can, or that you can't; you are usually right." —Henry Ford

"You must learn from the mistakes of others. You can't possibly live long enough to make them all yourself." —Sam Levenson

"If you want to be miserable, think about yourself, about what you want, what you like, what respect people ought to pay you, and what people think of you." —Charles Kingsley

"There are only two basic ways to establish competitive advantage: do things better than others or do things differently." —Karl Albrecht

"Talent does what it can; genius does what it must." —Edward George Bulwerlytton

"A great many people think they are thinking when they are merely rearranging their prejudices." —William James

"Forgiveness is not an occasional act; it is a permanent attitude." —Dr. Martin Luther King, Jr.

"You cannot build a reputation on what you intend to do." —Liz Smith

"Ninety percent of life is just showing up." —Woody Allen

"Smooth seas do not make for a skillful sailor." —African Proverb

"The happiest people don't necessarily have the best of everything. They just make the best of everything." —Anonymous

"You are not what you own." —Fugazi, American rock band

"A man is as big as the thing that annoys him."
—Albert H. Edwards

"No one can make you feel less of yourself without your permission." —Eleanor Roosevelt

"God looks at the clean hands, not the full ones."
—Publilius Syrus

"Don't forget until too late that the business of life is not business but living." —B.C. Forbes, founder of *Forbes* magazine

"Too many people miss the silver lining because they're expecting gold." —Maurice Setter

"An adventure is only an inconvenience rightly considered. An inconvenience is only an adventure wrongly considered."
—G.K. Chesterton

"I do not agree with a word that you say, but I will defend to the death your right to say it." —Voltaire

"If your number one goal is to make sure that everyone likes and approves of you, then you risk sacrificing your uniqueness and, therefore, your excellence." —Anonymous

"Always do right. This will gratify some people and astonish the rest." —Mark Twain

"The reason that worry kills more people than work is because there are more people who worry than work." —Robert Frost

"The task ahead of us is never as great as the power behind us."
—Anonymous

"A lie sprints. But truth has endurance." —Anonymous

"When you do not listen to your conscience it's because you do not want advice from a stranger." —Anonymous

"No one can be free who does not work for the freedom of others." —Anonymous

"Better to light one small candle than to curse the darkness."
—Chinese Proverb

"When in doubt, tell the truth." —Mark Twain

"You can observe a lot by just watching." —Yogi Berra's Law

"Never be afraid to try something new. Remember, amateurs built the ark, professionals built the Titanic." —Anonymous

"If you can't explain it to a six year old, you don't understand it yourself." —Albert Einstein

"You have freedom of choice, but not freedom from choice."
—Wendell Jones

"Truth is stranger than fiction, because fiction has to make sense."
—Anonymous

"I am not young enough to know everything." —Oscar Wilde

"Wise people talk because they have something to say; fools, because they have to say something." —Plato

"Find a niche and scratch it." —Anonymous

"He who praises himself has a congregation of one."
—Jewish proverb

"Everyone is ignorant, only on different subjects" —Will Rogers

"A critic is someone who knows the way, but can't drive the car."
—Anonymous

"Heads that are filled with wisdom have little space left for conceit." —Anonymous

"By the time your face clears up, your brain starts going fuzzy."
—Anonymous

"Perseverance is not a long race; it is many short races one after another." —Walter Elliott

"Let us so live life that when we come to die even the undertaker will be sorry." —Mark Twain

"When were the good and the brave ever in a majority?"
—Henry David Thoreau

"You are where you are today because you stand on somebody's shoulders. And wherever you are heading, you cannot get there by yourself. If you stand on the shoulders of others, you have a reciprocal responsibility to live your life so that others may stand on your shoulders. It's the quid pro quo of life. We exist temporarily through what we take, but we live forever through what we give."
—Vernon Jordan, in a speech at Howard University, 2002

"Adversity has the same effect on a man that severe training has on a pugilist—it reduces him to his fighting weight."
—Josh Billings

"Perseverance is the hard work you do after you get tired of doing the hard work you already did." —Newt Gingrich

"Nothing is more desirable than to be released from an affliction, but nothing is more frightening than to be divested of a crutch."
—James Baldwin

"The ultimate measure of a man is not where he stands in moments of comfort and convenience, but where he stands at times of challenge and controversy." —Dr. Martin Luther King, Jr.

"I try to take one day at a time, but sometimes several days attack me at once." —Ashleigh Brilliant

"Never let your head hang down. Never give up and sit down and grieve. Find another way. And don't pray when it rains if you don't pray when the sun shines." —Satchel Paige

"Paralyze resistance with persistence." —Woody Hayes

"Go out and preach the gospel and if you must, use words."
—St. Francis of Assisi

"If you must borrow, always borrow from a pessimist. They don't expect to be paid anyway." —Anonymous

"The character of a person is what he or she is when no one is looking." —Anonymous

"Lies circle the earth while Truth is still trying to put on its shoes."
—Attributed to Napoleon Bonaparte

"I not only use all the brains I have, but all I can borrow."
—Woodrow Wilson

"I have not failed. I've just found 10,000 ways that won't work."
—Thomas Edison, during the light bulb invention process.

"A leaky head never swells up." —Anonymous

"The rung of a ladder was never meant to rest upon, but only to support your weight long enough so you can reach for something higher." —Anonymous

"All that is not eternal is out of date." —C.S. Lewis

"Perseverance is failing nineteen times and succeeding the twentieth." —Julie Andrews

"We are drowning in information, but starved for knowledge and wisdom." —John Naisbitt

"There is a fine line between courage and craziness, and one between wisdom and cowardice. The people who drew those lines never knew the difference." —Anonymous

"There's no limit to what a person can do or where he or she can go, if he or she doesn't mind who gets the credit." —Anonymous

"I know God will not give me anything I can't handle. I just wish He wouldn't trust me so much." —Mother Teresa

"Pain is inevitable. Misery is a choice."
—Quoted by Christopher Reeves

"Hold everything in your hands lightly; otherwise it hurts when God pries your fingers open." —Corrie Ten Boom

"Contentment is destroyed by comparison." —Anonymous

"Success = those who are the nearest to me love and respect me the most." —Anonymous

"Some people like my advice so much that they frame it upon the wall instead of using it." —Gordon R. Dickson

"God whispers in our pleasures but shouts in our pain. Pain is His megaphone to rouse a dulled world." —C.S. Lewis

"Success in marriage is more than finding the right person: it is being the right person." —Robert Browning

"To solve big problems you have to be willing to do unpopular things." —Lee Iacocca

"We are always one generation away from total anarchy." —Anonymous

"Be kind. Remember everyone you meet is fighting a hard battle." —John Watson

"Truth is incontrovertible. Panic may resent it; ignorance may deride it; malice may distort it; but there it is." —Winston Churchill

"Anyone who does not believe in miracles is not a realist." —David Ben-Gurion

"Research is the process of going up alleys to see if they are blind." —Marston Bates

"Some people will pay their tuition, and then defy you to give them an education." —Robert A. Cook

"People defend nothing more violently than the pretenses they live by." —Allen Drury

"Travel is fatal to prejudice, bigotry, and narrow-mindedness, and many of our people need it sorely on these accounts. Broad, wholesome, charitable views of men and things cannot be acquired by vegetating in one little corner of earth all one's lifetime." —Mark Twain

"Never tell people how to do things. Tell them what to do, and they will surprise you with their ingenuity." —Gen. George S. Patton

"What we believe about God is the most important thing about us." —A.W. Tozer

"The person who makes no mistakes does not usually make anything." —Edward J. Phelps

"You can't hold a man down without staying down with him." —Booker T. Washington

"Our greatest weakness lies in giving up. The most certain way to succeed is always to try just one more time." —Thomas Edison

"The worst team in baseball's history won only 55 games. The best team ever won 110 out of 160, so you're virtually guaranteed to win 1/3 of the time and lose 1/3 of the time. The difference is the 1/3 in the middle. You don't know what bucket the game you're playing falls into, so if you're smart, you'll fight like everything for all of them."
—Tommy La Sorda (addressing Little Leaguers)

"The object of opening the mind, as of opening the mouth, is to close it again on something solid." —G.K. Chesterton

"Patience is the weapon that forces deception to reveal itself." —Coach Ken Woods

"Do not go where the path may lead, go instead where there is no path and leave a trail." —Ralph Waldo Emerson

"Work like you don't need the money, love like you've never been hurt, and dance like no one is watching." —Satchel Paige

"... I know what I have to do now. I gotta keep breathing. Because tomorrow the sun will rise. Who knows what the tide could bring?"

Chuck Noland
(Tom Hank's character in the movie, *Castaway*)

# ABOUT THE AUTHOR

Joel A. Freeman, Ph.D.—Accomplished author. Internationally sought-after conference speaker and workshop facilitator. Professional counselor. Success/business coach to executives. Behavioral analyst. Organizational culture-change specialist. Corporate trainer. Motivational consultant and mentor to pro athletes. Off-key singer and very bad dancer. Multiculturally astute. Photographer. Award-winning filmmaker. Passionate about dynamic, fun-filled excellence. A life motivated by curiosity. No Bull. No Hype.

Born in Maine (1954) and raised in a small town in Alberta, Canada, Joel A. Freeman brings a rich reservoir of personal experience blended with contagious enthusiasm, clarity, and down-to-earth humor to empower people from diverse walks of life with improved communication skills and maximized productivity.

The Freeman Institute®, of which Dr. Freeman is CEO/president, is a Maryland-based company with five arenas of expertise:

I.  Seminars, Workshops, Conferences, Presentations, Corporate Training, Staff Development.

II. Long-term organizational culture-change.

III. Executive coaching, specializing in Critical Incident Debriefings (CID).

IV. Cultural Awareness/Competency and Black History.

V. Entrepreneurship/Creative Business Implementation.

With a PhD in counseling, Dr. Freeman served as mentor/chaplain for the NBA's Washington Wizards (formerly the Bullets) for nineteen years (1979–1998). Freeman facilitates many seminar programs, including the popular:

—"Dealing With People Who Drive You Crazy!"®

—"A White Man's Journey Into Black History"®

—All Stressed Out and No One to Choke

—"Diversity: The Value of Mutual Respect"

—"When Strangling Someone Isn't An Option"

—"If Nobody Loves You, Create The Demand!"

Listed in Marquis *Who's Who in the World*, Freeman facilitates seminars with leaders in the federal judiciary, music and entertainment industries, corporations, government agencies, and heads of state of other nations.

The Freeman Institute® is the owner of an impressive black history collection (oldest piece dated 1553). Dr. Freeman has received rave reviews for his black history and diversity presentations. With well over 500,000 copies in print, Freeman's six books and three DVDs have received rave reviews worldwide, endorsed by Ken Blanchard, Bill Cosby, Julius (Dr. J) Erving, Les Brown, Brian Tracy, Joe Frazier, Ben Carson, and Billy Graham, and are published in twenty-eight foreign translations:

1. *Return To Glory: The Powerful Stirring of the Black Man* (book and film)

2. *Kingdom Zoology: Dealing With the Wolves, Serpents, and Swine in Your Life*

3. *Living With Your Conscience Without Going Crazy*

4. *When Life Isn't Fair: Making Sense Out of Suffering*

5. *A White Man's Journey Into Black History*®
   —123 minute DVD

6. *Professional Bloodsuckers: Dealing With the People Who Drain You of Your Time, Energy and Patience*
   —26-minute video.

7. *If Nobody Loves you, Create the Demand*®

---

Joel Freeman resides in Maryland with his wife, Shirley, and their four children, David, Jacob, Jesse, and Shari.

Dr. Joel A. Freeman
Box 305
Gambrills, MD 21054
Tel: 410-729-4011

Website: FreemanInstitute.com
Email: info@freemaninstitute.com

Additional Resources: at your local bookstore or online at WorkHardWorkSmart.com

- Four-CD Audio Book version: 5 hours, unabridged. Bonus—Includes the mp3 version of the entire book. Free download of sample chapters of audio book online.

- Next Generation Entrepreneur Clubs: Connecting Now with Later—Workbook (connects the contents of this book specifically to young adults, 15–26 years of age) —NGEclubs.com

- Entrepreneur Club Connection: Everything Relative to You, Your Business and Your Purpose in Life— Workbook (connects the contents of this book specifically to faith-based/non-profit organizations— emc2clubs.com

- WHWS.mobi: website specifically designed for cell/mobile phones (free downloads of sample chapters and ring tone of "Almost Reggae")

---

To book Dr. Freeman for a seminar or keynote address:

**Behind the Voice Agency**

Jan Smith

P.O. Box 1305

Franklin, TN 37065

Tel: (615) 599-9809

Fax: (615) 599-9801

Email: email@behindthevoice.com

# "A White Man's Journey Into Black History"®
### An Eye-Opening Experience That Transcends Race

---

"The knowledge I received this morning was stirring because [Freeman] related things that have long been accepted as fact and are supported by irrefutable evidence, yet have been muddled up in history."

"I was skeptical when I saw the speaker was white, but as he spoke, the knowledge and documented evidence was so powerful. [Freeman's] passion was captivating. All I want to do now is to share this information with as many people as possible."

"This was the best Black History presentation I have ever seen."
(EEO director of a government agency)

"The word 'truth-centric' hits the nail on the head."

### How You Will Benefit

- Visual & Verbal Tour Of Ancient Black History
- Understand the Significance Of Rosetta Stone And The Middle Passage
- 7 Tactics Employed In Blotting Out Historical Black Accomplishments
- What's Up With The Cover-Up?
- What Does A White Man Have To Say About Black History?
- What Is The Hebrew / Black Connection?
- Prejudice And The Grieving Process
- Tools For Mutual Respect, Dialogue & Hope
- A Message For Those Who Are Not Of African Descent
- Secrets Of Human Origin Uncovered By DNA
- How, When And Why Did Blacks Diminish In World Dominance?
- What Would Motivate A White Man To Be Interested In Black History?

### www.WhiteMansJourney.com

# Become a Digital Real Estate Mogul

## MultiWebConcepts.com

Your One-Stop Destination for Domain Names and More

### — Domain Names —

*Get new "dotcoms" real cheap!*

*Transfer your current domain names for even less!*

### FREE with every domain:

- FREE! Complete Email
- FREE! Forwarding / Masking
- FREE! Change of Registration
- FREE! Starter Web Page
- FREE! "For Sale"/ Parked Page
- FREE! Domain Name Locking
- FREE! Total DNS Control

www.MultiWebConcepts.com